Dowsing Wisdom

Change Direction...Change Your Life

Dowsing Wisdom

Change Direction...Change Your Life

(With the Swing of a Pendulum)

Dowsing Wisdom presents opportunities for release of outdated or irrational beliefs, new growth and inner peace. Let your Pendulum swing to show you how to find Joy and Happiness in life.

Helen Sladden

BOOKS

ISBN 978-0-9865840-9-1

Cover Design by: Doug Madden, Another MaddoG Creation
Typesetting and Design by Another MaddoG Creation

Contents

Dowsing Wisdom
Change Direction ... Change your Life

With the Swing of a Pendulum

Pendulums have been used in the past as a source of entertainment,
an aspect of psychic phenomenon,
or in a farmers search for water and minerals.

The book 'Dowsing Wisdom' provides a different opportunity to search,
find, and re-balance the energy surrounding the triggers and reactions to
uncomfortable life challenges.

Discover, Understand, Resolve, Achieve Inner Peace

And develop your Intuitive skills in the process.

Dowsing Wisdom Objective

Change Direction…Change Your Life

Learn to use a pendulum and
activate your intuition in the process.

Ask a few questions …identify the answers …
resolve the issues…find inner peace.

Once you release the blocks and resistances to change
you will be able to make peace with your past.

We are all entitled to live a joyous and balanced life.

May this process assist you on your path.

Acknowledgement

While this book has taken its time to be completed, I have immense gratitude for my family and the many friends and clients who have supported and encouraged me to keep going.

It is because of their beliefs in my connectedness and trust in my gifts and abilities to channel spiritual wisdom, that I am now ready to share this work.

A very special Thank You needs to be sent to Blaine, and Cheryl for their editing suggestions and support, and Doug for his patience and phenomenal publishing skills to bring this to fruition.

Thank you also to the Universe for the Guidance and channeled wisdom I have presented in this book.

Disclaimer

This work is for self-discovery, personal interest and entertainment purposes. The information contained herein is not intended to replace a relationship with a medical professional. It is not intended to diagnose, define, nor prescribe medical or psychological conditions, nor does it claim to prevent, treat, mitigate, or cure any such conditions. This work has been structured to provide an interesting and informative way to communicate with the deeper aspect of *Self* for understanding and potential clarification of certain issues. The publisher and author encourage you to make personal healthcare decisions based upon your own research and to seek partnership with qualified health care professionals when needed.

Readers Comments

This is a fantastic book that provides an easy, step by step guide to uncovering and often resolving issues by using a simple pendulum. I particularly enjoyed finding my answers in the various resources that the author channeled, which offer differing perspectives beyond what I had previously believed to be true. This helped me to get to the core of my personal challenges. I highly recommend this book to anyone who would like an easy to use method to delve deeper into their resistances to change and stumbling blocks in life. I have learned so much more about myself, and I do find my intuition becoming sharper. I am looking forward to her next work as a follow up: The 'Spiritual Alignment Experience' available on the author's website. I welcome the opportunity to participate in future workshops with her to gain even more insight. I am grateful that Helen Sladden has written this much needed book... Thank you! M. A.

Wow! Dowsing Wisdom has truly inspired me to pick up my pendulum and get back to trusting myself in using it again. Her explanations are simple to follow and the book flows from chapter to chapter. The Resources that she channeled (25 Categories for Reflection, 101 Life Lessons, 101 Core Beliefs, and more) and offers to her readers, are so appropriate, that I have had many 'AHA' moments. I just use my pendulum to find and read the one I need to understand the most. I know that this will be a book I will treasure and use over and over, not only for myself but for my family and friends when looking for answers and guidance. Life presents all of us with challenges and the author has given us a method to find answers to help work through them, to then let go and heal. May this work help you to find peace and joy in life again as it has for me. Thank you, Helen...Nat

When I was at a low point in my life, I was guided to have a session with Helen. Apparently she was a Life Skills Mentor, utilizing many of her energy healing and teaching techniques, to help open up, break through resistances and fears, then empower and teach her clients to do this for themselves. Her kind and gentle soul helped me to relax, and gradually find the importance of who I really am. Part of this process was to teach me Dowsing and Pendulum work. On my own, I was able to uncover events, blocked emotions, triggers and more that had been stopping me from enjoying life. When she first shared her work and now this book with me, I knew this was something she needed to publish for others. This book is beautiful and easy to use, and I refer to it often when I feel stuck or confused. The insights gained in Lessons or Core Beliefs, for example always amaze me. Owning the book is like having her with you on your healing journey. Thank you Helen: for empowering me, and continuing to support me on my life path ...Robert

Introduction

Preface

Dowsing can put answers at your fingertips!

*This book will show how to use a **Pendulum** to discover the path that is right for you and awaken your **Intuition** in the process*

Everyone's life is unique. No one else has walked in your shoes, looked at each situation or challenge through your eyes, felt emotions the identical way you do, nor has your specific history.

Whether one is looking for solutions to a troubling issue like a career change, difficult relationship, or a lost key or wallet, without knowing, we tune into the patterns or methods we used before. We automatically go back into our experiences and memories to seek resolution, or ask others what to do. The frustrating part in doing this is that most times we end up with the same result, falling back on our own existing pattern, helpful or not, and then wonder why our lives never seem to change. We pick the same or similar personality in a partner, stay in or find another dreary job, or just get a new key cut. Life goes on and we tell ourselves that someday things will be different or better. For those who have a more spiritual understanding, this simply returns our inner energy flow back to where it was in connection with the Universe. We then wonder why not only does nothing change, but why we fall back into re-creating a similar issue to work through again and again. There really is comfort in discomfort for some. It is what is known and deep down inside we haven't found the courage, faith or knowledge to know how life could be different, or, what it could possibly look like. For some people, the thought of change, stepping out and beyond what they know and expect is their biggest fear.

So, what needs to happen to actually step off the hamster wheel of our lives and find an alternative plan?

The answer may lay in how our conscious and subconscious minds work in keeping us safe and protected while still engaged in life. In simple terms: The subconscious holds all the rules, previous patterns, and terminology that we respond to, and allows our conscious mind to take care of the daily routines. It exists mostly as an autopilot - to provide what has gone before so life doesn't overwhelm or confuse us. What we need then is a way to bypass previous beliefs and methods to see a situation from a new perspective; potentially to obtain a different outcome. This in turn could stop the repeating patterns that make us question "Why did I do or say that again?" or "Why does this keep happening to me?" Dowsing, by using a simple device like a pendulum, and asking the right questions, can stimulate a fresh viewpoint, which in turn gives us more options and choices for a new or different direction than we have processed or traveled before.

My Focus

In writing this book I attempt to help you find possible answers to questions surrounding discomforts, irrational triggers and stumbling blocks keeping you from experiencing inner peace and joy. To do this, I have intentionally set this book to keep the process easy to understand and simple to use.

I will explain and define what Dowsing is when using a device like a pendulum, dowsing rods or body prompts.

Since 'Dowsing' actually means to 'search', I also will describe the various pendulum movements and swings that can occur when using it. These patterns are a result of and in answer to the questions asked and as a visual of your own subtle energy shifts.

You will also see that by using these tools and learning to bypass the questions of the intellectual or conscious mind, your intuition will begin to awaken.

In the Methodology, I offer ways to fine tune and develop your trust in the answers you will receive.

I will then present an opportunity to use your new found or reawakened pendulum skills in the Resources chapters. These were channeled to offer guidance, support, and encouragement. Once a specific answer is read and understood, it may present an opportunity to release and forgive yourself or others from the results and stigma of uncomfortable, or even painful and traumatic life events.

We are all entitled to live a life of joy, satisfaction and inner peace, defined by whatever those words mean to each of us. Although the path we take and the challenges we face may seem pretty rough and difficult at times, we are never really without resources and support to help us get to the next moment. The problem is that sometimes we just don't know where to look. My intention for this book is to offer you one method in which to find some answers and possibly take you one or two steps closer to this goal.

Please note that this work is merely an opportunity to explore options and different outlooks on particular issues. It is simply to inspire thoughts, offer new perspectives and potential release from old, outdated issues, emotions that never seem to shift, plus limiting behaviours and beliefs. I wish you success in moving forward into this exciting world of opportunity, inner peace and the beauty that does surround us.

If you are willing to look at life from a different perspective, Dowsing provides potential answers resulting in a new outcome for your life.

Namaste

Why Dowsing?

Intuition and Dowsing

Dowsing is defined as an act of searching.

Whether we have developed and trust our intuition or use a tool or device that is balanced for this, dowsing is simply an act as natural as taking a breath or feeling the heart beat. It can be defined as "an ability" inherent in every living creature, similar in fact to understanding the term "Sixth Sense". Intuition is the inner feeling, whether a gut response, skin sensation, or just a firm "knowing" that something around you is different, comfortable or needs to change. Dowsing, using a device like a pendulum or rods, could also be explained as the outward visual representation of what our intuition would tell us if we could tune in. In truth, the more in tune you become with dowsing in general, the less likely you will need external tools or pendulums for answers. For example, why do you sometimes cringe or feel the need to protect yourself when approached by someone before they say hello? Maybe you have felt a tingling in your hand or an unusual discomfort after picking up an object and quickly put it down. Most people don't recognize when this connection and subtle shift in energy happens. They talk about a vague feeling that caused them to hurry home, or a sudden prompt to cross the street for no particular reason, just to walk down the other side. They may laugh at an inner knowing when the phone rings as to who might be calling because they were just thinking of this person. It could also be recognized when you just don't feel right eating a certain food, and later feel ill, or by a sudden aversion to driving down a particular road that you have used many times before. Yet when most people think of dowsing, they think of a form of strange magic to see into the future, locate lost objects or divine below the ground for water or minerals using a Y-shaped branch.

However, this 6th sense is such a natural ability that even animals display this energy sensitivity. You see it when a dog instinctively growls and barks at a person it has never met before and yet happily greets and makes a fuss over another. It may happen as well when some birds or butterflies comfortably land on the hand of one person in a group but avoid others.

The term "Dowsing" actually means to search. A dowser then would be a person who seeks to discover something by recognizing a form of energy shift in or around them. There are many ways to do this. Some methods are as normal as noting and acting on your gut response when faced with a situation. One might also act on the body sensation of feeling physically pulled toward or forced away from something. This is called the sway technique, where we unconsciously or intuitively feel drawn towards something pleasurable and yet pushed away from pain or discomfort.

There is another method that is age old and uses a device such as a pendant, a needle on a string or rods that are designed to easily swing when directed at something and in answer to a question.

These tools have been used to search for lost objects, water or minerals below the ground, or just for fun to determine the sex of a baby before birth. The person holding this tool would ask a *"Yes"* or *"No"* type question and depending on the direction of the swing would receive their answer. It is interesting to note that in history books we are told that pendulums were also used during war time to locate hidden submarines, possible tunnels or areas for ambush by holding the device above strategic maps.

The pendulum when allowed to swing freely works as an outward display of a shift in energies that most of the time we are never aware of. We have all had moments when we suddenly feel the need to act or move. Fight, freeze, or flight are the extremes of these gut responses. However, there are softer, gentler nuances that sometimes we just miss or deny and then later have thoughts of "I did know better", or "I wondered at the time if I should". This connection is actually a result of the barely perceptible change in energy frequency that runs through everything here on earth. We can relate to this more easily when we think of the colour spectrum of a rainbow and how each colour that we see is defined by a particular frequency. In actuality, if we could physically see this frequency we could notice changes around us more easily. However subtle the energies are, we can still notice and relate to the shifts. For example, when things in our lives are going smoothly and we feel happy and content, our frequencies shift higher and the world seems to be a much brighter place. Yet when we are angry or feel lost and alone our frequencies shift lower and we actually say we feel down. Also, when we talk about the colours and relate to their coolness or warmth, we are simply referring again to their calculable frequencies. We say we are feeling blue or in the pink of good health, or when angry see red.

The change in frequency of the vibration is what is picked up by the pendulum simply by holding it in a particular way to allow it to swing. The energy shifts then are represented by various swings or movements allowing us insight we might not consciously be aware of. The tuning in method to dowsing sets this predictability. Therefore, depending on the direction of the swing, the intensity of its movement and the focus of the question asked, we can receive an answer we might never have consciously thought of. When the frequency is positive, clear and high, the pendulum, while being held, will move in a certain direction that will be opposite or completely different than when the frequency is negative or dense.

These changes between positive and negative represent the shift in relation to our energy, depending on the answer to the question asked. We feel them every day when we get excited or anticipate a happy event. We also feel the low ones when we are fearful or discouraged. The pendulum is simply an external visual to the internal prompts we all feel. So when using a pendulum, the differences represent the *"Yes"* and *"No"* answers based on the shift in energy frequency compared to our neutral energy or balanced and centred state. It can bypass our conscious thought process or subconscious belief system and shifts, depending upon the frequency the answer to the question generates.

It is important to note that true answers are never obtained if the dowser tries to anticipate the answer or wants it to be something that it is not. We can get in our own way, which is why it is so important to do this work from an impartial, neutral and centred state. Breathing, detachment, grounding, centering and protection are all important aspects to incorporate before undertaking a session. That way the energy shifts and nuances between answers are more easily discernible.

It is also vital to realize that answers obtained while using a pendulum are simply indicators of potential outcomes based on energy frequencies and information available at time of use. While the specific swings we are shown may offer huge "AHA's" and allow us to work through or clear issues or find objects and answers, **a pendulum should never be used to diagnose, treat or cure, or take the place of mental and health therapies.** Always check with a health care professional for your wellbeing. The purpose of presenting **Dowsing** in this book is to stimulate more trust in our intuitive insights.

To do this you will find various "**Resources**" included later on in this book for enlightenment and those "AHA" moments of release. These in turn can either allow permission to move through and let go of past hurts, the stigma of what we may have considered grievous unforgivable mistakes, or at the very least make some sense out of the nonsense that we call life. Uncovering outdated, non-productive belief systems or the lesson we feel we failed to understand at the time of the incident or issue, creates a sense of lightness in our energy. Taking a deep, freeing breath after each moment of discovery helps to anchor in the moment of closure or clarity. In the following chapter I will instruct on the simple way to relax with and use the pendulum. As you align with the pendulum work, your perceptions surrounding your own life plus those of others will heighten. You will also find that your intuition becomes more finely tuned as you begin to trust your instincts.

I wish you the best outcome for your journey, with support from the highest and best energies the Spiritual Realm offers, and for the greatest good of all involved.

Setting the Stage

Understanding the Process

Begin with Intent

In Spiritual energy work such as reading Tarot Cards, healing with Crystals, Spiritual Readings and Channeling, there is the possibility that a variety of spiritual entities of all frequencies will try to join in for the experience. In order to begin, it is important to set Spiritual parameters around this work. We do this by stipulating who is welcome in the session and who is not. This limits interference from opportunistic energetic influences. Therefore it is important to state that the session is to be for the greatest good of all involved and protected from any influences not from the highest and best energy realm in the Universe. There are many useful methods: prayers for protection and guidance, clearing the energy of the room with smudge, crystals or bells and asking for assistance from your angels and guides are just a few. To simplify this in my work, I set what is called an '**Intention**'. This is a statement I say at the beginning of each session. The purpose is to remove the need to repeat our desire for clarity, support and guidance on each subject or issue for ourselves, or others we might be working with. This sets the stage so that once we understand or have an answer to our question it will be for the best possible outcome, from the highest source helping us. Then the stuck or imbalanced energies can be released, to free us to move on in life and to the next question. If you choose to use this method of intention setting, once you are ready to start, read the following statement either out loud or to yourself. This makes it clear that when you say 'As per my Intention' in your work, this is what you intend and accept in support from the spiritual realm.

The Intention

"We ask for support, protection and guidance - only from the Highest and Best and for the Greatest Good. We ask the Higher Self and the Universal Collective Conscious to accept that when we say "To be released from this Being", we are asking for release from all energetic planes both physical and spiritual, from the Ego, subconscious and from any and all generations affected. In this asking, it is so, in light & love."

Begin at the
Beginning

The Place to Start

One step at a time

After you have set your intention and before undertaking any form of energy work it is essential that you do so from a centered place of inner balance. There are many ways to do this and even if you already follow a certain path to achieve this state, try the method below, and let's work through this together.

1. The first step will be to find a comfortable, quiet place to sit, maybe at a table so you can keep charts or notes and a glass of water handy, where you will be working with your pendulum. In energy work hydration is always important so remember to have a sip of water from time to time. With feet flat on the floor, take a few deep, slow, cleansing breaths and see yourself relaxing. Feel your shoulders coming down and tension around your jaw and neck releasing. Sit with your back straight and visualize the breath coming in through your crown chakra at the top of your head and flowing down through the spine, exiting out through your feet and base of your spine into the earth. Once you can sense yourself doing this, change the direction of your breath to come up from the earth through your spine and soles of your feet, cleansing and refreshing all that it passes through on the way up. Then believe you can breathe up and out through your crown chakra back to the Universe. This clears and cleans the chakras or energy centres as the breath exits out through the feet and crown at the top of the head. Now visualize breathing in from both the crown and earth at the same time into your abdomen, but this time sense your

breath exiting through your heart and solar plexus area. As the breath exits these two chakras, surround yourself with the sense of this energy as white light for protection and comfort. This is called centering and anchors the physical self between Heaven and Earth and will allow for more detached and less emotionally driven answers.

Once you have achieved this feeling of centred balance, make sure that you next offer a prayer of guidance and protection. This would be the intention we spoke about earlier. You can invite your guides or angels to be present to help, or those of someone you might be working with. You also need to re-state that only those spiritual participants from the highest and best and for the greatest good are welcomed. Just to repeat that in any energy work there is the possibility that a variety of spiritual entities of all frequencies will try to join in for the experience, so remember to stipulate who is allowed and who is not.

2. Next pick up your pendulum, which can be anything that dangles freely at the bottom of a 3 to 6 inch chain or string. You could use a favorite pendant for now, a suspended fishing weight, or an actual pendulum. At this moment the device is irrelevant as long as it can be allowed to swing freely. However, once you have mastered and are comfortable with the swings and are ready for delving more deeply into your issues, a metal pendulum will be more appropriate and unbiased in finding answers. While crystal pendulums are beautiful, they can add their particular vibration and frequency to an answer. For example, you are asking about a particular job choice that you know intellectually you will only hold until something better comes along. You ask your rose quartz pendulum is this job the right one. Since rose quartz is a crystal of

self love and forgiveness from the heart, it might answer no, because your heart really isn't in it. Your intellect and reasoning tells you it is available now and will help to get you to the next and better job. Which answer will you go with? This is why after becoming comfortable with the dowsing process a metal pendulum would be more appropriate and less biased in finding answers.

Hold the string or chain of your pendulum between your thumb and first two fingers and just let it dangle freely for a minute. Get comfortable with feeling the weight of it while your elbow is supported on the table in front of you. If there is no table then hold your arm to your side for stability with your elbow bent to allow the pendulum to hang freely from your raised hand. Find a comfort level in holding it out and away from your body. When you feel ready, from your relaxed and centred state, simply ask the pendulum to show you a 'Yes' swing. Be patient and simply allow it to move in some direction. Remember this is about tuning into an energy shift from a neutral state and not a demand to move. The resulting movement could be a straight line, oval or circle but the intention at this moment is just to let it move as it will. By repeating the phrase "show me a 'Yes' movement" in your thoughts or out loud, you are tuning in to any shift in energy that will give you a visual representation of a positive frequency. Once there has been some movement and at first it may just be slight... ask to be shown a 'No' swing. It may take a moment but the pendulum will move in a different direction to your request for a visual of a negative frequency. Some participants feel the difference between the two swings first inside their abdomen, or as a muscle twitch in their hands, before they see the change. Others are surprised when the pendulum appears to stop and then change direction. Be patient, as the changes of the swings can take a bit to get used to.

However the more you practice the easier it becomes for the conscious, intellectual mind to accept. Once you are able to stop the monkey mind chatter, or questioning thoughts asking if it will move, and letting yourself remain neutral, the movements will become stronger and more defined. It does take releasing the conscious mind from anything other than asking for a response to the '*Yes*', '*No*' request for movement.

3. Once the pendulum appears to shift between the two different directions, ask to be specifically shown the intended movement so you can define the difference between them. If the swing feels weak you can ask that it move with more power for now. This helps with building confidence and discerning the difference between the swings with more ease. Later, once the change between the swings feels more natural, the spontaneous intensity and duration of the swing will become important when receiving answers. Find within you a level of confidence in accessing the difference and intensity in swings. Practice until this feels natural.

4. There will be times when the pendulum takes a weird swing or won't move at all. When this occurs it means that you may have asked a confusing question, have no need yet to know the answer or there is not enough information yet to process an answer. This would be considered the '*Maybe*' swing and occurs fairly frequently during this work. It simply alerts us to rephrase the question for more clarity or look deeper into why the question is being asked. Remember there are no true shortcuts in life, especially when asking the Universe for assistance. Using a pendulum is simply an indication of a potential outcome. To be clear, the answers we receive are only based on the information that is available or that can be accessed at the time, due to the

specific wording of the question and the energies surrounding the request.

As you progress with pendulum work, you will find a connection happening, where you may almost anticipate a response before the swing occurs. This is simply your intuition developing. Remember that the responses you receive are based on changes in frequencies. As you start to notice this shift in your work, understand that you are tuning into your intuition. Learn to trust the feelings within yourself and identify where and how you feel them.

In addition though, as you continue and trust the shifts shown by the pendulum between 'Yes', 'No' and 'Maybe', you might also be shown optional swings. This does occur once comfort has been established with use. It feels as if the device has so much more to help you with and is asking for attention to other energy shifts you may not have been aware of. The movements may seem erratic at first but if you allow the flow, you will understand what is being offered. If you do notice it doing something different then you can ask questions as to the meaning for the change in swing. Apart from a "Yes", "No" and "Maybe" swing, you might find a motion that means you are on the right track but rephrase the question. Or, the opposite of that swing may mean you are totally off base, so ask the question from a differing perspective.

Swing motions that I have come across are circles both clockwise and counter-clockwise, or horizontal and vertical movements for positive and negative shifts. I also have experienced a combination of these depending on the pendulum I am using. There are others such as oblique movements, loops, ovals as well as flower petals, plus some combinations to indicate information from spiritual sources is being offered. The pendulum is truly an intriguing resource, once you align with it, through your balanced, centered and neutral energy.

5. It is also necessary to clear the energy around the pendulum from time to time. Running under cold water, using Reiki, or sitting the pendulum in sea salt overnight are useful methods. You will know when it is time, if you have used it for a while without clearing, as the answers may seem off or indeterminate. Just ask that the energies be cleared and give thanks for the work it does and you will be ready to use it again.

Mastering the Swings

Understanding the Answers

Now that you have practiced and mastered the *'Yes'*, *'No'* and *'Maybe'* swings it is time to begin asking questions.

At first it may seem silly, but ask the pendulum questions that you already know the answer to. This could be *"Is my name...?"* or *"Do I live in an apartment?"* *"Is my favorite colour...?"* *"Do I like a certain food?"* By doing this you can establish the swing more securely and also start to feel within your body the changes in frequencies that create the different swing responses. Do this a number of times until you build up confidence in experiencing the different swings.
Next, try asking more probing questions such as:

> *"Is my energy still in a balanced state?"*
> *"Have I worked hard enough yet to take a break?"*
> *"Is my desire for a specific outcome*
> *getting in the way of an impartial answer?"*

As long as the questions are formed to receive an answer in a *'Yes'* or *"No"* format, the pendulum will give you a response. Please keep in mind this is simply a tool or device to define shifts that occur in the frequencies of the energy planes in and around each of us called the Etheric Planes. The planes are energy rings that spiral around each of us both internally and externally and encompass our Physical, Mental, Emotional and Spiritual bodies. They extend and vibrate at our own individual frequency, depending on our circumstances, beliefs and experiences. They project out beyond our physical selves into the world around us where we interact with others and internally to the core of our being. The shifts that the pendulum will pick up are the changes in the frequency caused by our reaction or response to situations and experiences in our life at that moment. When we are in alignment with a certain truth or expectation, our frequencies are balanced and we feel peaceful. Yet when we are upset or challenged and find life difficult, then our frequency shifts to a lower vibration and we get stuck. The answers simply indicate what an outcome could potentially be, based on where your frequency is in that moment. If the answer isn't what you would like, then question yourself as to what you can do or change within your routine or responses to create a more acceptable answer. Nothing is ever carved in stone where energy work is concerned. It is possible if you change one thing that is predictable about you (the time you eat for instance, the route you take to work, or your routine in the shower) then like dominoes falling, you immediately can alter an outcome. Using the pendulum is actually like being a detective. Yes, you will receive answers. However, if they are not what you thought they might be, go back and revisit why you are asking the question and what needs to happen to make the shift for a better outcome.

Some of you may wish to ask questions about or for other people. In this instance there is a distinction between asking **about** and **for**. To ask questions on behalf of or for other people is ethical only if you have their express permission to do so. To ask about other people is unethical unless you are strictly asking questions in relation to your personal interaction with that other person. To invade the energetic privacy of another individual without permission may have undesirable consequences for the person asking the questions or using the pendulum.

At other times you may try to ask for winning lottery numbers, or the outcome of a bet, and since there is a great vested interest in beating a system, which involves the ego, there can be no guarantee of accurate results.

Record Keeping

Why this is important

It is also useful to keep a journal with the date and time of day that you are doing this work. Record the swings you have for yes, no and maybe and the type of pendulum you are using for future comparison. Also if there is an odd swing or two, record that as well with the question you were asking plus the answers for future reference. Sometimes, the swing will be really strong and you will know beyond a doubt you have the right answer for that moment. Sometimes the swing is only moving slightly in one direction or another, so stop and think what in your life could change to make it a stronger or more definitive answer. You might also decide to alter the question or revisit it at another time or on another day. The question you are asking may also need to be simplified or made less confusing. Simple explanations may also be interfering with the answers, such as not being centred before you start, taking a quick moment while waiting for a phone call, or not having had enough water to drink. It might be that there isn't enough information to answer the question, or you have no right to know the answer. As they say, practice makes perfect, so keep the pendulum and notes with you to use often and it will actually feel like a friend after a while.

Please remember that the pendulum is only a device to explore answers to work with. It isn't the solution to a problem or a diagnostic tool. It is simply a device that can be used to obtain better understanding. Once you have your answer, take the time to see if there are any thoughts, memories or feelings that occur surrounding that answer that might be helpful to let go of, resolve, accept or look more closely at.

As you regularly work with the pendulum, you will also find that you become more sensitive to the nuances in change around you. You might notice a mood shift in a friend during a friendly discussion, or have a more definitive internal feeling as a response to a situation or issue. All that is happening is that your intuition is opening up and responding to the changes in energy around you, with people, yourself and your environment. Record these thoughts and sensations along with the prompts you may have become aware of. You will also note when you are off balance and find yourself realigning, and breathing from your centre automatically. This again is healthy and helpful to do, so that you can see when life is off balance in other areas around you. We all have a "sixth sense" or intuition, but it takes a bit to develop it and trust in that innate wisdom. The pendulum is a simple tool or vehicle to show us how we can relate to and engage more positively with life. The simple swing externally will eventually become an intuitive knowing or feeling inside that we may spontaneously act upon as we learn to trust.

Probing Deeper

Learning to Trust

Once you have mastered the different swings and are comfortable holding the pendulum it is time to ask different types of questions. You may wish to know an outcome, or a time frame for a project. There really is no limit to the questions you can ask, and as you become more comfortable with the process, asking becomes easier. The only restriction to the questions for now as we progress through the initial stages of this work would be that you ask ones that require a *'Yes'* or *'No'* answer and be for your own edification. Asking on behalf of others is wonderful if you have permission, but asking about other people is an invasion of their right to privacy, unless it is related to something about self. Be careful as in all energy work: What you project is what eventually comes back. Always make it be for the greatest good as well as from the highest and best energetic support available.

To get you started, here are some random sample questions. Record your answers and at a later time revisit these questions to see if anything has changed. Once you get a feel for the swing, I am sure you will find a great number of areas you might like some insight into. Practicing also helps to heighten the awareness of the shifts in energy you may feel in and around you. You are starting to awaken your intuition, so if you also feel an inner prompt before the pendulum settles on a swing, record that feeling as well. In energy work, it seems the more we open to trusting spiritual support, the more support we are given. Create a list of your own questions pertaining to different aspects of your life and see what information your subconscious is willing to share. Be clear and specific in the wording to receive the most likely 'Yes' or 'No' response. Remember if the pendulum is inconsistent with its swing, then clearing might be needed, or reformatting of the question. The other reason could be not enough information at this point to give a firm answer or you are just not supposed to ask the particular question.

Is this the right time to move?

Am I on the right track with this decision?

Am I balanced today?

Would this group be good for me to join right now?

Are my thoughts being influenced?

Do I challenge myself enough?

Am I just being lazy?

Do I get angry too easily?

A method for finding answers to these next two questions will be highlighted in the next section.

What needs to happen to stop this repeating pattern?

Do I have enough information to clear this issue?

What to do with the Answers

Going beyond 'Yes and No'?

'*Yes*' and '*No*' answers are enlightening, and sometimes all that is required to understand, let go and move on. Bringing things to our awareness helps us to make decisions and find clarity surrounding some issues. However, there are times when a simple yes or no doesn't suit our need. Our lives are not simply based on '*Yes*' and '*No*' answers, although as children those two words became firm boundaries for our safe and comfortable existence. To live within those parameters meant peace in the house, at school, as well as acceptance. The difficulty only occurs when we don't or are not allowed to challenge the rules as we grow and simply continue to abide by them. To highlight this, as you matured, did you still have to hold the hand of an adult every time you crossed the street or were in a parking lot, to be safe? It is often interesting and a bit humorous once we have created new and more mature guidelines, to reflect on the things our parents told us as children. Some of these beliefs and rules are still of value, and we pass them onto our own children as traditions, or acceptable behaviours. But, past programming can be outdated and the need for some of those parameters long since gone. Remember that our subconscious has diligently protected and stored all this data from the beginning of our existence. So, unless we alter those programs, we become predictable and complacent in our attitudes and responses. We only realize this when we start to ask the question of **why** our life never changes. Our subconscious can only offer the old and accepted path we took to be safe, as that is the only information it

31

has stored. It can never realize there are other options available until we find a way to change the programming and be open to accept new options. Sometimes when our lives feel stuck or blocked, or we have resistance to change, one of the reasons could be the very same rules and beliefs that kept us safe as children. We may physically mature but somewhere deep inside we still might abide by the influences others placed on our security and acceptance.

Then there are times of shock, fear or trauma, where we imprinted a promise, action or new belief of what had to be done to merely survive. The subconscious would also store this information in case we were ever faced with a similar situation. These become our unconscious Core Beliefs which we automatically act on when challenged in similar ways. However, these spontaneous actions can also create limitations, discomfort and restrictions in our daily existence. The need for the promise or belief may have passed but the response to those emotions remains tucked inside.

Next I present an opportunity for deeper reflection and further understanding. The Resources following in the next few chapters were channeled through me on behalf of my clients. I needed a way to help them identify their buried or blocked emotions, lessons to be learned and or outdated beliefs that were keeping them stuck. Change is difficult for most but when it becomes actual resistance, or emotions seem to overwhelm and our lives are ruled by insecurities and fears, we need to find an alternative way to view life.

Introducing the

Resources

Universal Guidance:

Introducing the Resources

Before I explain how to use the next chapter, it is important to note that all of these Resources are merely suggestions to think about, and see where or if they apply. They do not define or diagnose a medical or health issue and are not to be relied upon to replace regular and consistent professional, medical and psychological health care. If you do uncover a deeply troubling issue that isn't easily resolved, seek professional support. The suggestions offered through the Resources are simply alternative ways to look at situations and challenges. I hope they help you find inner peace to return to a more neutral and balanced energy flow.

Please have a notebook and pen handy to record the thoughts and feelings that arise to allow for greater clarity and potential for change.

In order to benefit from this next section, it is important to remember that if a person finds themselves stuck, emotionally blocked, or facing similar issues repetitively, the seed which produced the root or roots (repeating patterns) of whatever caused the discomfort or inability to move freely forward, <u>happened in the past</u>. It was a potential moment in time when there was no comfort or resolution, which in turn now taints or colours the decisions we make and even the way we view life in general. Fears, anxiety, irrational anger and the value we place on the person that we became, may be tied up in unresolved past experiences and perceived mistakes we made, due to the influences we had at the time. Insecurities and irrational beliefs can start at a very young age by the simplest of actions or criticisms and judgements that may or not have even been directed at us. People, places and the experience itself can influence our future direction, decisions and beliefs. This then may create the limitations and blocked or stuck energies that cause us to repeat issues or hold ourselves back from our true self. Some of this is self imposed to allow us to keep going past the pain or embarrassment. We may choose to minimize our existence and feel if we are invisible and unobtrusive in life, no one will expect anything from us. The opposite could be to act aggressively, push others away, or become controlling and insensitive to those around us. Behaviours, attitudes and beliefs are learned through the results of our reactions to experiences, as well as the controls and influences imposed by others to have us conform to a life style or belief. Remember if others are unhappy with your ideas to change or create something new or move in a different direction, then they are impacting upon your right to freedom of expression, actions and joy. Should they try to interfere with your potential, then it would be wise for them to look inward to their own insecurities and imbalances. We are all unique in our own way with the right to be free to live with purpose

For the average person, when faced with an uncomfortable or life altering situation, there is always deep within a need to understand and ask "what just happened?" and "why?" When the answers, support and encouragement are not there for immediate resolution and when issues simply do not make sense, we tend to create a way to exist (Core Belief). We may make promises to ourselves so we can get to the next moment. We tell ourselves we really are ok, when we are not. We hide behind bravado, become the class clown or learn to manipulate a truth as a survival technique. After all, life continues and we must find a safe and comfortable way to carry on. This is exactly where buried emotions and the sense of being stuck may begin. We find ways to survive, get by, and make it to the next moment. We also pray that what occurred will never repeat itself, or that someone else might never have to go through what we just did. We push it aside, swallow it, deny it, change it around in our minds for more comfort, but never get to the seed that spawned the root to resolve it.

This journey, through the Dowsing experience to find our Inner Wisdom, using the resources provided, is meant to enlighten a person through logic and understanding. When we can step back and become an observer, free of the stigma or emotional impact of that moment in our history, we just might be able to let go and heal. Think how you would feel without guilt or unresolved anger, for example. If you could dissolve and heal an insecurity issue, find the personal power within to stand strong in who you are and not what others believe you to be, how good would that feel? In being able to do this, it removes the personality or persona that was created for protection, a desire for rebellion or to fit in or possibly to simply resist change. Once we realize the past is just that: part of our history, and we get to the initiating seed of the issue, we are offered a new way to view those events. This begins a journey into self-worth and confidence. By taking the personal sting out of the issue or circumstance, forgiving ourselves and others, learning the Lesson we missed or releasing an outdated Core Belief, we can free ourselves to fully engage in our passions and life. Then we can adopt a new perspective, courage and freedom to accomplish the things we have hiding deep inside, and find the passion and joy life has waiting for us.

Please remember that with all self-help tools, the following resources are meant to stimulate thought and see things from an alternative perspective. The "AHA's" that may happen are certainly freeing and enlightening, but are never intended to take the place of professional, medical and psychological support.

Presenting the 5 Resources

Which one do I choose?

The **first** resource to get you started is a list of 25 Categories. As I have said we are not always consciously aware of why we feel stuck, bored or seem to face certain events over and over. By holding the pendulum over each number and asking if this is something to look at, it will move to your 'Yes' answer when the most important item is discovered. If it moves to a 'Yes' signal over more than one, then ask for the most relevant one to be defined. Later you can go back and see what the other identified category(s) had to offer. Read what has come up and record your thoughts. See how it might apply and follow some of the suggestions.

An additional idea, when you are ready, would be to go through each category, one day at a time and see how balanced you are in each one. To make this exercise be of more value, record the events at that moment in your life, with the date and your issues, joys and feelings. We don't always recognize our stressors or frustrations in the moment until we are forced to stop through frustration, fatigue or potential illness. Doing this, will offer you an idea into your ability to find peace in spite of what is currently happening. Our lives and circumstances are always in flux, so one category that is balanced today might be something to relate to on the next day. Ultimately, we are here on earth to learn, grow, make a difference and support each other.

This way we not only make a better more peaceful place for all, but also find within ourselves a sense of calm and inner peace. Be the change you wish to see in the world first, and you never know what options quickly become available to help you.

The **second** resource is a list of **52 Obstacles** that may seem insurmountable. Again, allowing the pendulum to swing when it hits the one that applies can be eye opening as we really are the ones in our way. We might also have allowed others to define our ability to live peacefully or move forward toward our own goals. Ask yourself why this obstacle is stopping you, how this affects your outlook on life, and what you can do about it. Is it really insurmountable? Do you need to ask for help with this issue? Would talking to a person involved help to clear this obstacle? When you identify, work through and remove an obstacle, similar to eliminating a large rock in the garden, you have room for more options to flourish and grow with freedom and joy.

The same is true for the **third** resource of **52 Motivators**. While we know we may stop ourselves and often create obstacles in our path, through indecision fears or insecurity, this category offers a Motivation to actually get going. It is always good to see why we aren't achieving something and then to find a motivation or reason to do so. Select one and then think what you might be able to do if you held onto that particular motivator to simply get moving and start. Motivation at best holds our attention and becomes a goal to achieve and yet at the very least is a reason to get off our butt and simply begin.

The above two resources often go together. If there is an obstacle in life, then the motivator list may give the push needed to try again. Think of them collectively as a way to understand what is stopping you and a potential reason to get moving.

The **fourth** resource is a series of **101 Core Beliefs** that we tend to live by. Most of the time, we are oblivious as to why we act the way we do. We have become complacent, and predictable in our responses. This is great when we are on top of the world and our circumstances and challenges seem to resolve easily. We believe the world is an abundant and benevolent place and that we are on track accepting life as it unfolds. The difficulty begins when it is a challenge to make decisions or we feel held back, stuck and fearful of change. We find ourselves repeating things over and over and wonder why. We can't find an answer and then justify why we do what we do, because we fall back into believing our own truth. The problem with that scenario is that if the belief was only based on survival, getting through the moment in time, and not on thriving, then we remain stuck, or irrational in our thoughts. Remember it could also be something imprinted to keep us compliant and safe as a child, which now no longer applies. When a Core Belief has been identified by the *"Yes"* swing, ask that any negativity surrounding this be removed. Do this by holding the pendulum and reading the statement involved. Allow the pendulum to simply swing until it stops. It will move counter-clockwise at first over the statement. Once it stops, then while continuing to hold the pendulum, read the answer to the statement that follows right below. You will find the pendulum starting to swing yet again but in the clockwise direction. The pendulum movements in this case are related to identifying the imbalance caused by the belief. The first movement (counter-clockwise) will be used for removing the negative, maybe outdated energy by allowing it to swing while reading the statement. Once the pendulum stops swinging, it will then start to swing in a clockwise direction as you read the positive affirmation below the statement. I will explain this swing technique in the next chapter, but a quick explanation is that the pendulum can also tune into the vortex of energy that surrounds all things. By moving in a counter-clockwise direction first, it is able to neutralize and throw off the darker, outdated or negative energies. However, the Universe abhors a vacuum, so the replacement positive energy will cause the pendulum to swing in a clockwise direction filling the void that was created with unconditional love and light .as well as the positive suggestion,

The **fifth** resource comprises a list of **101 Life Lessons.** We are often told that Earth is the biggest school house and every day we are in situations to learn or possibly teach and inspire. We may ask our self in times of confusion, what am I supposed to know, or what did I miss that I seem to be going through a similar incident again and again. If we could tune into our intuition during those moments, we would have a greater understanding or wider perspective on the event taking place. We might even say "AHA" or "how did I miss this?" These types of responses can only happen when we are impartial or removed from the incident as an observer. If, when questioning what needs to be known, the pendulum indicates to look for a lesson, be open minded. My experience has shown that possibly the entire reading of the lesson is needed or, only a part of it makes sense, and at the very least you will find a phrase or word that will trigger a response of awareness. It is interesting that occasionally the same lesson may come up a few times while we explore various aspects of it.

41

Resources and Pendulum Activity

Swings for Choice

Importance of the Swing Technique

Now that you have mastered confidence in your pendulum activity, the first question is to find out if any of the Resources are needed for healing and clearing at this time. Simply ask if there is something for you to know as you name each section. Sometimes more than one Resource is indicated as the collective information can help explain and create a bigger picture. Once this information is identified by the yes or no swing, narrow down the search by asking again, '*Yes*' or '*No*', is this the one appropriate for me to start with? Once noted, you also can ask if there is more than one item necessary within each Resource. Record these findings as you go. Our thoughts can take us off on a tangent, causing us to forget where we started or what else needs to be addressed. Keeping a written record as you go eliminates the potential confusion and keeps you on track.

Since holding the pendulum over each number to find which ones are applicable will take forever, the following instruction is the easiest way to access the information .in all the resources categories. To find the correct number regardless of the Resource choice indicated, hold your pendulum still and then ask in groups of 10 if the number needed is in that group. The phrasing would be: Is the number included within 1-10, 11-20, 21-30 and so on. Once the pendulum indicates by a yes movement, that the group of 10 you addressed is the right one, then break it down to groups of 5. For example, if the group of 10 is in the 40's, ask if the number is included within 41-45. If it says no or doesn't move then count 46, 47, 48, 49, or 50. If it indicates yes in the first 5 of the group immediately ask about each number as you count up. Always stop the pendulum and confirm the number chosen by asking if this is correct, before proceeding.

While using the pendulum when reading and releasing any imbalances pertaining to the resource, there will be times when it will start to swing, gaining in speed, or slowing, only to speed up again, repeating this cycle until it comes to a stop. The first reason for this is that as humans we are much more than a simple physical being. We are personally surrounded by levels or planes of energy called the Etheric bodies. These energy rings are located both internally within our physical self and externally, by layers or planes stretching out into our energy field. The external ones are why we might know a person is lying or unwell when they say they are fine. It is the imbalance or discordance in the other persons' Etheric energy planes when it interacts against our own balanced frequency that we pick up on. We identify them as the Physical, Mental, Emotional and Spiritual planes of our existence. Because the pendulum works using the shifts in energy compared to our balanced and neutral state, if we ask for a clearing of negativity, then the pendulum will access all layers unless otherwise instructed. Therefore, the Pendulum Swing Technique is a healing movement similar to one that is used in Reiki healing sessions. This energy spiral or vortex exists around us all the time. Phrases like "swept off our feet", "spinning out of control" or "carried away" are unconscious references we use. As an example, have you ever seen the sand on the beach eddy and swirl around when the wind picks up, or snow spiraling on the roads as it begins to lightly fall? We are not really conscious of the ebb and flow until we feel off balance and talk about our equilibrium being off. So, when asking the pendulum to identify a 'Yes' or 'No' answer, we simply are asking that it show us the variance in frequency when compared to our neutrality. We can further ask after we remove the energy that we replace the energies to bring balance back so there is no void in our energy field.

When asking for the removal of any energy not wanted or unhealthy, negative or destructive in our Etheric rings or fields, internally and externally, the pendulum will swing in a counter-clockwise direction. This is similar to hurricane force winds that throw everything up in the air and out of the way of its path. The intensity of the swing and the number of times it ebbs and flows will indicate how deep the imbalance was or how long it has been stuck in your field. Once this is done though, and the pendulum comes to a stop, it is imperative to ask to replace and fill the void with positive thoughts, suggestions or the desire you have in mind for a better outcome based in love and light. Letting go of what is outdated, harmful, or obstructive to our current wellness, from the seed of the issue and on all levels of our being is only the beginning of healing. Replacing and rebuilding the energy with unconditional love and acceptance, forgiveness and more is needed to continue the healing.

The next chapter begins the section on Resources.

Author's Note   Opportunity

Once you feel confident in your Dowsing skills and if you are interested in going deeper for understanding and closure, I have created a discovery work book that utilizes the resources in this book. These questions, charts and suggestions help in redefining this work, for your own use or with others. Issues such as buried emotions, resistance to change, past Life Events, anxieties, fears and phobias, irrational angers and repeating patterns are just a few of the areas that can be worked through. This compendium is available on my website: www.DowsingWisdom.com in e-book format.

In providing this Channeled work, Dowsing information and question format, I have been asked by many to offer a practitioner training course. There are those who understand that in helping others we are in fact healing ourselves. This is intensive and hands on, explaining why particular sections and questions are pertinent to digging deeper for more information for healing and release of blocks or buried emotions. I offer answers and suggestions to make this not only interesting work, but inspiring and healing for all participants. We are all looking for Inner Peace, Balance and to live in Joy. Releasing the outdated and no longer necessary prompts, beliefs and habits from the past allows us to live a more fully engaged and wonderful life. I have also been asked to provide separate workshops for those simply interested in delving deeper. If you have specific requests for consideration please connect by email. I look forward to creating a community of like minded spiritual seekers. For more information email Helen@DowsingWisdom.ca.

Thank you.

Categories for Reflection

25 Choices

1. *Physical Body*:

Our physical body is a myriad of complex parts. From the organs to the musculature, the endocrine and circulatory systems, plus the neurological and alimentary system, the list is endless and seems daunting to break down for healing purposes. However, many books have been written to describe the energy connection within the individual parts for a better understanding of what we need to do to resolve or support our greater wellbeing. Louise Hay is a wonderful resource when looking for the energetic reason to ailments or discomforts within our bodies. For example, when people are feeling fear or anxiety, they will mostly feel these in their stomach area first. The clenching of the gut which makes breathing an issue, or nausea and indigestion may happen. The reason is that our stomach hosts these emotions. How many times have you heard someone say that they can't stomach something or swallow what is going on? Another example could be when faced with shoulder issues. If you look at what is going on in your life you find that you are carrying heavy burdens that seem without resolution. Have you even known anyone who faced gallbladder issues and you could see how bitter in life they had become? These correlations make it easier to understand why certain areas of the physical body are calling out for attention. In energy work when the physical body finally breaks down, it is usually the last effort to get our attention to change. If you were honest with yourself, you would remember thinking things like, I haven't been eating properly lately, or I can't keep going with so little sleep, or maybe I should do some exercise and deal with my stress. These are all inner prompts asking you to take care of things before they reach the physical level where there is no longer an option to be ignored. Take a moment and examine your physical health and see why this prompt came up. What intuitive message or messages have you been ignoring or what physical ailment could be explained by an energetic imbalance to allow for faster healing?

2. *Faith and Beliefs*

In this section you are being asked what you believe. Some feel there is nothing but the reality of what our senses or science can verify. That is great if there is comfort with this choice. Others feel there is an all encompassing energy watching over and helping us. This as well is terrific as long as this brings a sense of peace and well being. The issues begin when we feel lost, alone and isolated not only from the things we would like to have but from people who love us or are at least willing to help. Some admit to being mad at God or the Universe, feeling that their prayers are not answered. Others take on a feeling similar to 'what is the use', this is all there is and I can only depend on myself. Ultimately what we choose to believe in will be reflected in how we live life. If what we believe suits our purpose and we live a productive, respected and happy life supported by those beliefs then there really is no issue for concern. If though, one is unsettled or unhappy within oneself, it might help to ask whether deep down you truly believe or desire that your life could be better. If the answer is yes, then ask yourself what is missing or needs to happen to make it better. Create a goal sheet with achievable time frames and take action. However if the answer is no then it is time to seek help to discover what it is that is interfering with your right to joy and inner peace. Pendulum work

51

is neither the diagnosis nor the cure. It is only an indication based on an energy frequency that shifts within our bodies to help us to better understand ourselves and our thoughts.

3. *Centered/Grounded*:

Because we are simply embodied spiritual beings, our physical presence is what keeps us earthbound by gravity. So to work with the energies and feel the shifts we need to be totally present, anchored and yet centered between earth and Universe. Once we have that strong connection to earth we also need the strength of our spiritual selves in alignment to feel the nuances and subtle changes that become the answers to our questions. So then, grounding is about being earth connected. It is great to feel this strength when we are faced with a challenge or situation where we need to find our courage to see us through. Think of a Martial Arts competitor who plants their feet while their opponent tries to force them off balance. However, for this work we need more than grounding. Since we are spiritual beings in a physical suitcase, it is important to find our centre between heaven and earth. To do this if you haven't learned how, you need to bring in both earth energy through your roots (feet and base of spine) and also at the same time spiritual energy through your crown chakra at the top of your head. These then meet within your abdominal area to be able to vibrate out into your energy field. You can do this by seeing or believing you are breathing in through both your crown and roots at the same time into your abdomen. From there it is a matter of letting your breath out through your heart and solar plexus to surround yourself with unconditional love and light and make the centered connection. This does feel different and less heavy than being grounded and is a state that many strive to find in meditation or when doing healing energy work. From this place of peace, balance and neutrality your answers will be less likely interfered with by your hidden fears, desires or expectations. If your pendulum has chosen this area to reflect upon it might be asking you to re-center yourself or delve deeper into what is taking you off balance. Then you can reflect upon your options of what to do.

4. *Emotions*:

Being human we are bound to experience hopes, fears, sorrows and joys and anything in between, or a mixture to work through all at once. Life can be filled with wonder and awe yet also filled with pain, frustration or trauma. Part of our earth journey is to have these experiences to learn from and grow and possibly understand enough about them to help others. When life seems good and we can work through our challenges and make peace with our more negative or darker emotions then you will probably not be drawn to this category. It is when we get stuck in destructive thought patterns, or hold onto the darker emotions of fear, frustration, anger, etc. and seem unable to find the joy in life, that we are asked to take a closer look to resolve them. Using your pendulum over these suggested emotions, identify the one or more you are drawn to. Then think about how these have impacted your life and where and when they might have started. See if you are willing to resolve or move past them.

Emotions Table

	Emotion A	Emotions B	Emotions C	Emotions D
1	Abandonment	Exhaustion	Lazy	Rudeness
2	Abuse	Feelings of failure	Loss of confidence	Sadness
3	Anger	Fears/phobias	Loss of innocence	Safety or security issues
4	Anxiety	Frustration	Loss	Selfish
5	Betrayal	Gloom and doom	Low self-worth	Self-loathing
6	Bullying	Grief	Lying	Self-pity
7	Confusion	Guilt	Meanness	Shame
8	Cowardice	Hate	Mentally lost	Shock
9	Control	Helpless	Mistrust	Spiritually disconnected
10	Death	Hurt	Obsessive	Stress
11	Deceit	Immobility	Obstinate	Stubborn
12	Depression	Impatience	Pain	Tension
13	Disappointment	Inability to speak up	Panic attacks	Timid
14	Discouraged	Inconsolable	Pride	Terrors
15	Divorce	Indecisive	Procrastination	Unmotivated
16	Doubt	Inflexible	Rage	Unreliable
17	Embarrassment	Irreconcilable	Rejection	Weary
18	Emptiness	Irritable	Resentment	Withdrawn
19	Envy	Insecure	Restless	Worry

5. *Thoughts:*

We have all heard the saying that your thoughts create your reality. Or, as you think so you become. Focus for a moment or two on what your internal voice is saying. Is the constant chatter in your mind making you feel good, supported, appreciated, loved, and encouraged, or does it bring you down. Do your thoughts offer you inspiration, new ideas, solutions to problems or more discouragement? If you are drawn to this category then find a way to alter the negative thoughts with what you can do, and have achieved and not of what you can't have or hasn't worked. Even by focusing on the smallest success or blessing, more gifts and surprises will follow. However the same is true that if you only focus on what doesn't work or what you don't have you also will end up with less.

6. *Communication:*

This section requires you to look at how you verbally interact with others in your life. Do you speak more than you listen? Must you be heard every time or can you keep some thoughts to yourself? Does it always have to be your way and do you need to be right all the time? Can you admit to your mistakes or offer help and consolation to others? Must you be the centre of attention or are you the mouse that sits in the corner wishing you had the courage to speak up for once. How we communicate in the world by both speaking and listening or through painful or determined silence says a lot about our character. Are your opinions welcomed and readily discussed? Or does it seem people try to shut you down before you really get going? Think about your interactions with others and find a balance between listening, speaking, the importance you place on being heard, as well as simple and respectful silence.

7. *Behaviour/attitudes:*

We have all heard that our actions speak louder than words. We may deny acting out or having a chip on our shoulder but in this section you are being asked to look at the opposite of this. Simply put, are you aware of how people respond to you? Do you have a large social circle? Do friends and family call you at the top of their list to join an event or function? Or, do you find out later that a party had taken place and friends or family may say they didn't ask you because they thought you might be busy? How others respond to you is a good indicator of how your behaviours and actions are defining your acceptance amongst others. When unresolved hurts and emotions are ruling our life, our behaviours can become defensive, aggressive and even argumentative. Ask what needs to happen to find the inner peace that allows you to be calm and respectful of others. This radiates an energy that attracts others to include you in their lives.

8. *Responsibility:*

What does this mean to you? Are you someone who feels the burden of others on your shoulders? If so, who put the burden there? Are you really responsible, or is someone allowing you to fix their life while you juggle the things you need to do for yourself? Do you take responsibility for your own actions, thoughts, and deeds? Or, do you find yourself deflecting and laying blame on those around you rather than looking at your part in the circumstance? If you have been drawn to this section, you are being asked to re-evaluate your position in your own life.

Sometimes when we repetitively take on the responsibilities of another's well being we are actually stifling or denying them the right to make their own mistakes or learn from the ones they have made. Take a step back from what you do and worry about on a daily basis. Decide who owns the issues, who created the issues that are causing the burdens and who actually needs to take action to resolve them. Be responsible for your share and allow the other people involved to own theirs. Ultimately the one person we need most to be responsible for is ourselves. Once we have found balance and made peace with our strengths and limitations, we can then offer to assist others from a firmer and more supportive foundation. This allows them to learn, grow and heal, without interference and judgement, resulting in others finding and achieving their confidence and strengths.

9. *Connections/Influences*:

If you are drawn to this category, you are being asked to take a look around you. Who is in your circle of life to support and encourage you? Alternatively, who do you support and encourage? In a balanced world both of these situations would be very comforting and satisfying. However, some of our connections can be more demanding, selfish, opinionated, and controlling. They stay in our lives if we do their bidding but disappear when we would like to be heard or supported. Some people may want you to do things you are uncomfortable with and that may interfere with your well being on all levels of physical, emotional, mental, and spiritual. Our own thoughts can also influence how we live our lives. If we drag the past up in arguments or refuse to forgive or seek to resolve issues from the past, these will also influence our viewpoint on life, and the right to a peaceful and stable existence.

By using your pendulum you can ask where you need to look or what connections you need to re-evaluate for a happier and more satisfying life and then work either on your own or with help to clear them.

10. *Integrity/Honesty/Commitment/Excuses*:

Do you say what you mean to say and mean the things you do say? Do you follow through on your promises, or make excuses when something better comes along? Are you truthful in your relationships and always honour your commitments? How you live your life is a message to the Universe of the things you value and want more of. So if you do want relationships with people who value integrity and honesty and those who are able to make and honour commitments then you must first be this person. Instead of offering excuses or ways to avoid commitment, commit yourself to following through on choices in life and see the difference this will make. In order to be respected by others we must first learn to respect and love our self.

11. *Intentions/Goals*:

Without a destination it is really difficult to start or plan for a holiday. Without a desired outcome why would anyone take on a challenge? If you have always wanted to drive a new car, but never investigate the price, or options available then how would you know when you could afford or find one? If you have been drawn to this section then you are being asked to create goals and set intentions for change in your life. What have you dreamed of doing or owning? What interests have you not yet had time to pursue? By setting intentions and creating achievable goals, and then breaking them down into steps that you can follow to reach them, the Universe will happily become your partner simply by enhancing the energy you are expending and creating opportunities.

12. *Relationships:*

This category asks you to look at your daily interactions with family, friends, co-workers, neighbors, people of authority and strangers that you may bump into. You are being asked to check in with yourself for your authenticity in these interactions. Do you present yourself as real, engaged and present or do you just smile and nod when they speak? Do you take over a conversation, appropriately respond or change the subject if it doesn't interest you? Are you able to offer assistance when needed or asked, or do you simply say that although you could, you are just too busy right now? Are you really too busy to help? Do you freely join groups and share honestly, or do you sit back and wait for others to coax you, or wish to remain invisible? This is a very interesting category to examine due to the fact that until you have a very real, honest, and trusting relationship with yourself, it will be impossible to share these qualities with others.

13. *Forgiveness... To Give and To Receive...To Let Go*

Forgiveness is one of the hardest challenges we face. Most feel that if you forgive a person then you let them off the hook and they might do whatever it was again. In reality, forgiveness is about coming to peace within yourself about an issue that was either done to you or that you may have perpetuated. If you hold out and remain angry, hurt or bitter then in reality you are the one stopping your life from moving forward. Forgiveness has nothing to do with forgetting. We learn from everything we do and stockpile this information to protect ourselves from falling into the same trap or re-experiencing the same pain over and over. To forgive and accept forgiveness is to actually remove yourself from whatever the event was so that you can see it with different eyes, learn from it and become strong again in spite of it. We all make mistakes and do things we may not be proud of. It is really time to let go and heal by forgiving our self or offering and accepting forgiveness to and from someone else. Most of all once you can forgive yourself your life will become more peaceful and less judgmental.

14. *Challenges...Life Path or Ego Adventure*:

We all face challenges on a daily basis. Some are fun, like where to go for dinner or what movie to see. However, decisions about family, health, career and anything that feels uncomfortable can potentially interfere with our carefully structured lifestyles and cause upset, anger or insecurity. You are being asked to look at the challenge you are currently facing in terms of what it is bringing to your life. Is it simply causing drama, creating the need for recognition and support? Is it something that you have been ignoring and now cannot be pushed aside any longer? Could it be something that you can learn from and maybe once you have succeeded in rising above it or found the solution to, could help others on their journey? Challenges are actually our way to learn, progress, and develop self-worth. The problem arises when we stay stuck by our ego in the challenge, wanting attention or someone else to create a solution for us. Asking for help when needed is not the issue. Intending that someone else will provide the rescue only suggests we will have to repeat the challenge in a different way if it was part of our journey to learn from.

15. *Personal Expression...Creative Outlet:*

Everyone needs to be recognized as an individual at some point in their lives. This could be by being a good friend, loving mother or father, good student, employee or boss or other such scenario in life. However satisfying this recognition may feel, this category is asking how you express yourself and your personal need for self recognition. In the terms of energy, we all have a Sacral Chakra (energy center) that lies slightly in front of our spine just below our naval that oversees our personal expression, self love, plus nurturing and creativity. If this chakra is not exercised through creative expression (dance, writing, art, colours, nature, exercise, photography etc) and self nurturing (care and consideration and time out for self) then we find ourselves incapable of being grounded. We then tend to deny our need to be seen or heard, and look for love and validation from others to replace what we have the right to give our self. What have you done lately by taking the time to simply validate and show love to yourself? What outlet for your stress or self-nurturing have you pursued? Practice some form of personal creative expression and look to your needs for comfort and health on a regular basis and you will find yourself more peaceful and healthy inside with more energy, compassion and patience to share.

16. *Self-Worth:*

If you have been drawn to this section then you are being asked to look at the value you place on yourself. This isn't about what you can do or have accomplished. It also isn't about comparing yourself to others around you. Yes there are rich people in this world as well as people living on the street. This section though is asking you to determine how you feel about yourself when there is only you looking back from the mirror. Where do you fit in the world with the level of self-worth you own? It is about the feeling deep down inside that you know your worth when it comes to achieving your expectations. If we place little value on ourselves then it would seem we are always waiting for validation for the things we do and if we don't get any then we feel worthless until we try again to get recognition. If we over value ourselves then our ego gets into the action and our expectations become too grandiose. When this happens we can blame others for our lack of success or wear ourselves out trying to grab the brass ring of life. It is important to be real with ourselves. How much value do you place on yourself? It is not about the amount of money in the bank, the accumulated possessions or the number of friends. It is about the feeling deep inside that you have worth in this world and are able to wake up every day inspired to make a difference. Simply being the best that you can be is all that is asked for.

17. *Self Reflection... Spending Alone Time*:

It is important to pause in life and take time out by yourself. Put away the work to be done and books to be read and chores in front of you and simply sit with yourself quietly in reflection. Take the time to sort out the important things from the busy things. We can get so caught up in dramas and turmoil and lose sight of the peace that helps us to heal and be calm. You are being asked to sit quietly with yourself removed from phones and TV and lists of things yet to be done and just relax in quiet meditation. Listen to you inner self and get a sense of what is best for your wellbeing and not what always needs to be done to help everyone else. Re-evaluate the important things in life for you. Most important though is to find an inner peace at least once a day out of the chaos that can surround you.

18. *Stress*:

Ok, so you have pushed yourself to the limit. The ceiling feels like it is falling in while the ground below is caving in. Nothing is making sense and the more you do the less you can accomplish. You are exhausted and weary, and you know you need to stop, but just don't know how. What do you need to do to first acknowledge that there is actually stress in your life? Then how do you relieve the pressure from all the demands on your time or the need to find solutions to the problems? Although stress can be a great motivator, it can also be a root cause for disease. You are being asked to take time, acknowledge the distracted or frenzied feelings and find a pleasurable way to release the pressures building up within.

19. *Sleep Patterns*:

Sleeping is essential to mental emotional and physical well being. It is time out for the body to recharge and heal. You are being asked to evaluate how well you sleep. If you seem to dream a lot and wake up then it would be helpful to keep a journal of your dreams. These can be signals or messages from your subconscious as to solutions to problems or areas that need to be supported. If you toss and turn, or wake frequently and find it difficult to sleep, then you might ask yourself the areas in your life you are avoiding or the ones that are troubling you. If there are changes in your sleep patterns then it might also be wise to have a medical check up to see if your body is trying to tell you something. There is no set answer as to the number of consecutive hours of sleep everyone needs. As individuals with varying life situations and needs, when we are healthy, balanced, satisfied in life, and productive, our sleep will be natural and nurturing. It is when the pattern is interrupted or changes, that it would be wise to examine why.

20. *Money*:

What are your beliefs about money? Do you have enough? Do you get by? Do you over spend and then pray to win a lottery? Have you put money aside for your future? Or do you work so hard to save it that you have forgotten how to take time out to have fun? Do you fear losing what you do have and keep accumulating and never spending just in case something happens? Money is a difficult category because a lot of what we feel about it was influenced by our upbringing, country of origin, religion and challenges that we have had to face. If our families came through a tough time, or we are from families that didn't have much, our thoughts would be focused on how little there is. If our parents were savers and thrifty, we would believe we must always work hard to put it away as there might never be enough. The other side is also true. If our youth was based on wealth and we were given everything we wanted, then to work and accumulate new money might be a difficult task. Money as a tangible object was simply an original form of energy exchange. Value was set by the seller and the buyer then had to offer something of equivalent value to receive it. It would have been difficult to put 4 chickens in your back pocket to buy the grain your family needed, so currency became more portable with ascribed value to various coins. To fear it or revere it, puts far more emphasis on this object of currency than is warranted. Seek to become neutral to the energy surrounding it, and as you relax your hold it will flow more easily both to you and away from you as energy needs to do. You will discover that accumulating it and also using it will become part of a daily practice. In this neutral manner, saving for a particular goal is also easier and faster when the energy surrounding the money is natural without an emotional component. Make peace with your finances. Challenge yourself to view them impartially to seek balance in achieving goals, clearing debt, investing in your future and saving or spending.

21. *Work/Career*:

Are you satisfied with the direction your life is taking when you look at your career path or work path? When you recognize that the majority of your waking hours are invested this way, you are being asked to check in with your satisfaction levels of doing what you are engaged in. Is it work that you can leave behind at the end of working hours so you can focus on family, a social life, self nurturing or further education? Is there room to progress or be inspired? Can you work your way up in the company, or take other courses while there to further you income making ability? Or, does being there day after day stress you, and depress you? When you go home do you simply need to spend time alone away from others that might want your time? Is it affecting your health in any way or your relationships? These are focal points to consider if this category has come up for you. If the answers are more negative than positive consider what else you might like to work towards and start making those plans now.

22. *Interests...passions*:

Do you feel that your life is focused on everyone else and you have forgotten who you are? Maybe you are busy with family, friends, work, or your time is taken with health issues or trying to get by financially. This section asks you to reconnect with yourself and simply ask what it is that you are most passionate about. What cause can you help with or what interests have you lost touch with that you would have loved to have pursued? Remember that although you are connected to others by life circumstance, relationship and choice, you are still an individual with desires, hopes and goals. It is time to reconnect with what inspires you. Take the time to reignite your passion within yourself. You will be a much happier individual with stress from everyday challenges less likely to have as big an impact as before.

23. *Personal Growth/Education/Exploration On All Planes*:

We know that we are spiritual beings here on earth having a human experience. We also have many layers or planes as they are called of energy that shift and flow as quickly as our thoughts and emotions. These Etheric planes are listed as the physical, mental, emotional, and spiritual layers of our existence. As such we are here to explore through them, learn, delve into mysteries, create new ideas and pathways and enjoy the adventure that cannot happen anywhere else due to the duality earth provides. So, the question in this category is what are you doing to expand your knowledge, share your ideas, or create something new for the heck of it? Have you tried a new dance step, cooking foods from a different country or a different genre of music? If you are retired, have you thought about taking a course or studying, or experimenting with a new hobby? We are here for a short time and death at some point is guaranteed. What will you accomplish, support, resolve, learn or create to contribute while you are here?

24. *Unresolved Trauma/PTSD*:

Many of us have had moments in our lives that have shaken our faith, trust, belief and security. It is unfortunate but it does happen. We may have buried the memory, or still experience nightmares. Maybe there are flashbacks or triggers when certain smells, sounds or words are spoken. We may have either shut down, feel fearful or become aggressive in our thoughts and actions. If you have been drawn to this category, then it would seem it is time to face the horror, tragedy, or circumstance and seek a way to heal from it. To allow something that happened in the past to still control your present and alter your future is far too much of your power being given away. If you have survived something terrible, painful, hurtful, embarrassing, or worse, then you are being asked to seek guidance, and/or medical support to make peace with the issue.

25. *Gratitude/Blessings*:

We have all heard that our thoughts create out reality. You are being asked at this time to check in with your own thoughts. Are you focusing on issues and problems and the things that are worrisome? Unfortunately, once your thoughts centre on what you don't have or doesn't work or the things you feel are wrong in your life, you seem to only see more of the same in the world around you. Start to appreciate the little things that do go right. Someone holding a door open for you, or a stranger offering a 'good day' greeting and a smile. Maybe simply feeling the sunshine on your face for a moment because you can, hearing a song you like, or the smell of baked goods when you are out shopping.

Once you can focus on what is good and appreciated in your life, things will shift to allow you to see more of what you do have and what can work. The attitude of gratitude as well as counting your blessings is more important than you have yet to realize.

God grant me the serenity to stop beating myself
for not doing things perfectly,
the courage to forgive myself
because I am working on doing better,
and the wisdom to know that you already love me
just the way I am.

Author Unknown

Obstacles and Motivators

Obstacles

1. I procrastinate

2. I don't want to be singled out

3. It feels like too much work

4. I am too depressed

5. I just don't care

6. I don't have enough money

7. My results are never fast enough

8. I don't want to do it alone

9. I am disorganized, confused and indecisive

10. I enjoy the concept but not the work involved

11. I am unable or reluctant to prioritize

12. I am hiding behind fear

13. I suffer embarrassment, shame or guilt for doing something outside of family acceptance

14. I feel inadequate or weak

15. I am not smart enough

16. If I succeed people will want even more from me

17. I find it easier to let someone else take the lead

18. I don't want to make a mistake

19. I am too complacent

20. I never had to struggle before

21. I am caught up in lies and have lost the truth

22. I don't know where to start so I can't plan or set goals

23. I wear too many masks and don't know who I am

24. I don't feel worthy

25. I lack focus

26. I am just not interested

27. I am afraid I will be losing something

28. I can't give myself permission

29. It's not safe.

30. I don't want to be wrong.

31. I have never had a reason to believe in myself.

32. I lack self-confidence

33. I am unwilling to change

34. No one cares what I do

35. I am too sad

36. I always let myself down

37. I am just too angry

38. It takes courage that I don't have

39. Nothing has ever worked for me before

40. It just hurts to even try

41. I never learned to speak up

42. I don't trust

43. I don't know how

44. Learning something new is too hard

45. If I succeed then something else will go wrong

46. It's easier not to try when I know I always fail

47. I am a disappointment and a mistake

48. I lack tolerance and patience

49. I have too much pride to suffer being wrong

50. I hate myself

51. I can't let go of my negative thoughts

52. I am just empty inside

Positive Motivators:

1. To walk in the path of others who have achieved greatness

2. Realization and completion of long term goals

3. To find and identify my true self

4. Being the first to innovate a new idea or concept

5. To share or teach knowledge and wisdom

6. To challenge myself to complete or find a solution that was not apparent before

7. To discover legitimate proof and implement change to defeat a skeptic

8. To see myself achieving a larger goal by succeeding at smaller steps

9. To be happier

10. To achieve personal success

11. To heal or create better health

12. To become financially secure

13. To be at peace with myself

14. To become confident

15. To re-create self-worth

16. To develop self-esteem

17. To prove I am right

18. To create a better life

19. For praise or validation

20. Curiosity

21. To be accepted by a particular group or society

22. To be a leader or an authority and to make a difference

23. To heal and resolve personal conflicts to inspire and motivate others

24. To be a mentor or role model

25. To be stress free

26. To find inner security and peace

27. To stand in my own power

28. To be able to make my own decisions

29. To resolve conflict within the family

30. To let go of my destructive and negative thoughts

31. To take action

32. To be more pro-active and less re-active

33. To learn from my mistakes

34. To make peace with my grief and sense of loss

35. To stop holding onto anger and resentment

36. To stop sitting on the sidelines

37. To stop doubting everything

38. To become more tolerant and accepting of others

39. To stop fear from holding me back

40. To approve of myself and not look for approval from others

41. To be more responsible

42. To embrace both my strengths and weaknesses

43. To let go of excuses

44. To let go of the need for control

45. To stop worrying about everything

46. To let go of my pride and become more humble

47. To stop feeling like I have to prove myself

48. To stop being the rescuer all the time

49. To learn I have the right to say NO

50. To stop rejecting myself

51. To accept my strengths and limits and stop driving myself so hard

52. To know I only have to be good enough for me

Core Beliefs

9

101 Core Beliefs

1. *I am nothing, I have nothing and I will never amount to anything.*

Every day I discover ways in which I am unique and different. As I explore my own interests and focus on the things that I enjoy, I see that I have the freedom and power to achieve any goal I choose.

2. *There is nothing to like about myself, why would anyone want to be with me, I don't want to be with me.*

I like who I am, and the more I accept myself and love myself, the more I have to share. Accepting and loving me first is the key to attracting others into my life.

3. *I am powerless to stand up for myself.*

I am stronger than I give myself credit for and the strength I need to achieve anything I desire is already inside me. It is up to me to make time to practice exercising my strength of will. By doing this I will gain confidence in myself and respect from those around me.

4. *If I can make someone else happy first, then I will be happy.*

It is important for me to be happy first then I will have more to inspire and share. It is a waste of my efforts to try to make anyone do anything they have no desire to do. The state of happiness is a personal choice for me to experience first and then will radiate out through my energy and simply become contagious.

5. *I am filled with shame and guilt and am not good enough.*

I have allowed shame and guilt to hold me hostage for too long. Only I can choose to keep feeling this way or choose to let them go. When I decided through circumstance or choice in the moment to feel guilt or shame, I forgot that I have the power to embrace those feelings, really look at the cause, and resolve the issues to then move on. It is Ok to let go, forgive myself and allow balance and peace within. The goodness I feel within myself is not to be compared with anyone else as I only need to feel good enough for me. I am not responsible for others reaction or response to my truth.

6. *I am unlovable.*

I am worthy of love. When I find ways to love myself first, I will be able to accept and appreciate the love others have for me. Only to the amount of love I do have for myself, can I attract that level of love from others.

7. *I am self-centred and self-serving and do not deserve the goodness in life.*

My selfish actions have caused me to feel resentful, and isolated. I realize that when I embrace the opportunity of focusing on others my self-worth increases. This outward support and generosity from my heart when given without expectation becomes a magnet for unexpected rewards.

8. *I am always wrong.*

Everything I do is an investment in me for my tomorrows whether I succeed at first or not. I am now free from judgement to experience life regardless of any and all outcomes. Being wrong at times is a necessary part of life and learning and when I focus more on the times I succeed, I will realize truly how often I am right!

9. *The way others treat me, proves I am worthless.*

What I believe about myself is reflected in the way I am treated by others. As I value myself and know that I am worthy of respect, this will be what is then reflected back to me. I am responsible for teaching others the way I choose to be treated.

10. *I can't trust anyone or anything in my life.*

Trust for others comes after forgiving and loving me first. By trusting myself I will know where and on whom I can place my trust.

11. *I am afraid to fail and afraid to succeed so I won't even try*

Simply making the effort to get started will give me courage to do more. The end result is not the issue; the commitment to myself to make the attempt gives me strength and satisfaction.

12. *I don't really know who I am.*

I know I am an equally important individual with my own path and purpose to learn and achieve something here on earth. I now intend to use sacred alone time to explore my interests and passions to find and embrace this new me.

13. *I am unmotivated and have no strength of will to complete or achieve anything.*

I am excited and ready to try new things and like exercising a muscle, I will get stronger and more adventuresome as I complete or achieve each task. When I set a goal for something that I really desire, and give myself a time frame, I can challenge myself to succeed.

14. *I never have anything of value to say.*

I am confident when speaking my truth. In the past I chose not to speak or join in. I now find that the thoughts I do have are worthy of expression and when I speak with honesty and purpose I am listened to. The more excited I am about my interests the more I will have to share.

15. *I only trust what I know to be true, change is too frightening.*

The world and everything in it is constantly changing. I am excited to increase my knowledge and explore my options outside of the limits I have placed on myself. By doing this I will be able to embrace the opportunity to experience and create change.

16. *I will never have anything I actually want, I am not good enough.*

I am tired of holding myself back and getting in the way of receiving the things I choose to have. I am worthy of having exactly what I ask for, and I am open to accepting something even better.

17. *I am alone in this world and even God doesn't want me.*

I know God loves me more than I will ever know or understand and when I believe this to be true I am never alone. As I accept and love myself, my energy changes and others find it easier to approach me to create lasting, healthy and honest relationships.

18. *I always disappoint.*

I realize that by trusting my inner self I have a lot to offer. I always do the best that I can and never intentionally let myself or others down.

19. *I will never be perfect.*

Being perfect is a myth and unattainable as it is judgement based. I only have to be good enough for me.

20. *The world is a large, frightening and unfriendly place.*

I don't have to look at the whole world, only my part in it. I am unique and here to make a difference by following my path.

21. *I always feel I must defend myself, my words and my actions*

In the past I have allowed myself to live by the judgements and criticisms of others. I never felt I lived up to their expectations, trying to fit in, yet always letting others down. I now realize that defending myself and my right to be me is holding me apart from enjoying the real essence of who I am and the things I like and believe in.

22. *I am insignificant and have nothing to add to the world.*

When I find joy in the things that I do I give positive energy back to the world. My positive attitude may simply be the inspiration that helps save a life or provides motivation. I don't need to 'do' anything; I just choose to 'be' a positive influence.

23. *I am to blame for all the bad things that have happened to me and must never talk about them.*

I believe in myself now and realize that others may have said or done things to me in my past that made me feel responsible. I now free myself from their control, viewpoint and suppression and allow forgiveness and acceptance for the things I cannot change into my life. I am also free to speak my truth at any moment I choose.

24. *Lying and manipulating to get my needs met is easier than being truthful.*

I realize that the manner in which I treat others around me, invites that treatment back to me. Lying and manipulation may have seemed like an easier path, yet it is also a path to self destruction and disrespect. Being truthful with honest intentions is simply the better path as the truth once spoken never needs to be defended.

25. *If I get strong and self-reliant no one will pay any attention to me.*

I realize my weak state holds me hostage and brings unwanted judgement to me. Becoming confident will free me to achieve more in life. By being self-reliant, others will trust and believe in me. By always being the best that I can be I will attract others that work equally hard to make a difference in this world.

26. It seems the happier I get the angrier the people around me become.

I am entitled to live with happiness and joy in my life. If others have a problem with my positive attitude it is more about their inability to experience their own joy or share in mine. I do not have to make myself miserable or feel guilt because life is going my way.

27. Anything less than aggression shows weakness.

I realize that aggression creates power struggles and control issues. When I am assertive I speak with strength, confidence and power from my soul. Being aggressive actually suggests weakness within that is a deflection, whereas being assertive in your actions and words suggests a confidence and strength in your personal power.

28. I am stupid and never have anything to offer anyone.

When I find ways to know and understand myself and make myself happy first, I find I have so much more to talk about and share with others. I have definite likes, dislikes and interests that are important to me, so I am not stupid. My experiences can be the inspiration or motivation to help others create change.

29. It is safer to be alone than let others get to know me.

I am a unique individual with many ideas, gifts and talents to offer. Not everyone may appreciate what I do or what I have to say and that is their choice. Yet, by believing in who I am I will find security, confidence and satisfaction in my life. I will also be respected by others as I strengthen my respect for myself.

30. *It is easier to give up or give in.*

Giving up and giving in gives the power of who I am to others. It is an excuse I have used to avoid engaging in life. By taking a stand as to my beliefs and opinions, I feel better about myself, and I can then make a difference in this world.

31. *My stress is bigger and stronger than I am.*

I am using stress as an excuse. Stress is a normal life experience and can debilitate or motive me. When I accept stress as a challenge to overcome or resolve, I find strength and confidence in myself.

32. *The more I do and give to others the more they might like me.*

I do not have to buy love and support from others. When I find ways to invest first in myself, then I can make wise choice as to what others may need and not burden them with my insecurity of needing validation or attention.

33. *I must have done something to deserve what is happening to me.*

I realize that things happen for a reason. Believing that I am to blame or that I deserve the outcome defeats my ability to understand the issue and choose a path to resolve it. It is not always about me! The interactions that I have with other people and the situations I find myself in are opportunities for personal growth for everyone involved. Knowing this, I can be open, allow others an equal share in the experiences and create a more positive future.

34. *I avoid challenges so I will never make a mistake.*

Mistakes are simply opportunities for personal growth and a way to know more about myself and the surrounding world. When I face the challenges in my life I open up to new ideas, people, and opportunities as well as the chance to share my perspectives and beliefs. If I continue to avoid challenges I will never know what I am truly capable of.

35. *I am not strong enough to help myself.*

It is up to me to find ways to strengthen myself physically, spiritually, emotionally and mentally. No one can do this for me. As I put my efforts into discovering 'one' thing that I 'can' do for myself, my strength, confidence and ability to do more will grow. By helping me first, others will be more willing to offer assistance when I really need help.

36. *If I jump in first and control everything then I know it will be done right.*

There is more than one 'right' path to achieve a goal. By stepping back and observing how others do things, I am open to different perspectives, ideas and opportunities. I will also inspire others to share, learn and change.

37. *I don't know what my purpose is and can't set goals.*

I will find my purpose when I step out of my comfort zone and engage in activities that challenge me to learn more about my likes and dislikes. By discovering and then pursuing my interests, I will begin to feel an inner drive to make a difference, inspire others or give birth to something that creates change. Once I find a focus that brings me joy, goals are easier to set and obstacles to achieving them disappear.

38. *I just can't be myself because no one will like me.*

Looking to others for approval and validation stops me from enjoying my life. It is my life and I am entitled to my likes, dislikes and interests. If others cannot accept me as I am then it is not for me to convince them of my worth. When I find ways to like myself I allow others the opportunity to know the real me.

39. *I was born unlucky and taking risks is not something I am willing to do.*

Luck is a state of mind. I have always been as lucky or unlucky as I chose to be. By using luck as an excuse I refused to engage in the natural process of trial and error. I now invest the time to resource potential outcomes for any risk that interests me and by doing this I strengthen my ability to succeed. Every risk provides opportunities for personal growth. Whether I fail or succeed as an end result, I will always achieve something along the way through the experience. Luck has really nothing to do with it. My intention to learn and experience does.

40. When something happens I always focus on the worst possible outcome so it won't happen.

By focusing on worst case scenarios I am attracting negativity and undesirable outcomes. To expect the worst and be relieved by something slightly better limits the Universe's ability to offer amazing insights, and opportunities to me. I now allow for the best possible outcomes at all times.

41. I refuse to make decisions because people will expect me to follow through and act on them.

By taking control of my life and acting on decisions that I have chosen for myself, I become stronger, more confident and find it easier to set goals and celebrate achieving them. By refusing to decide and commit to a path, I have actually made a decision to keep myself back from engaging in opportunities life might offer. I refuse to allow the perceived or real expectations of others dictate my choices and decisions for my life.

42. I have to be better and try harder than others to constantly prove myself.

I am of equal importance to every other living soul regardless of their abilities, gifts or talents. To motivate and challenge myself for the purpose of being a better me is the true ideal and is all that is required for my life. To constantly compare myself and try to best others for praise or validation will eventually exhaust and undermine me.

43. *Everyone is smarter than me; I will never amount to anything.*

I believe in my ability to know what is right for me. I have value through my experiences, talents, gifts, and interests. If there is something I am not sure of, do not understand or wish to know then I am confident enough to search for answers. I am the only one comparing my intelligence to others and putting limits on myself.

44. *If I criticize and judge myself first, I won't feel so bad when others judge me.*

I release myself from self-criticism and judgment. I increase my self-worth and the value I have for me by loving and forgiving myself. I identify my strengths and weaknesses and realize no one needs to be perfect. I am a unique individual with goals, interests, gifts and talents. When I know I have done the best that I can, regardless of any outcome, I lose interest in the opinions of others.

45. *Only if I prove myself by hard work will I receive praise. I can't take time for fun.*

I am the only one who needs to approve of what I do. Working for praise suffocates my true nature and puts a limit on my personal growth and understanding. As I complete each task or achieve each goal to my own satisfaction, I will give myself permission to celebrate me. By taking time out for fun I re-energize my strength, belief and faith in my ability to be the best I can be.

46. My life will be just like the others and I will get sick and die young.

I am a unique individual and simply because others in my life had a difficult time or health issues and died young, I realize that was their journey and choice. I am not them. I enjoy maintaining my health and well-being, and refuse to be compared or linked to others. I am entitled to follow my own journey to complete the purpose I came to earth for.

47. As long as I am in control I will never be surprised and I will always be safe.

Life is about change and challenge. The need to control all aspects and find all answers first in my life so surprise never happens, limits opportunities through unexpected life experiences. The element of surprise offers new perspectives, excitement and choices to make following my purpose or path more interesting. It is always a choice as to how I view surprise. By engaging in the unexpected that life offers, I build inner feelings of security, courage and strength.

48. I am so afraid of making the wrong decision it is easier to never set any goals, then I will never be a disappointment.

By not setting and achieving goals, I am only really disappointing myself. The number of decisions I am allowed to make in life is without limit. If my first choice fails to satisfy my needs then I can easily and simply choose a new course of action. It is my life to live and is entirely up to me to make it the best I can.

49. If I always tell people what they want to hear I will never get into trouble.

Finding my voice and speaking my truth is now most important for my inner well being. To tell someone what they want to hear to avoid trouble will actually cause trouble when the truth is finally asked for.

50. I am alone and unworthy of being noticed or supported. It is easier to be alone, so no one will judge me.

It is now more than ok to be the most important person in my own life. I will commit to being the best that I can be for myself first. I am the one judging myself and keeping myself alone. It is time to make peace with who I am for myself first. When I stop judging myself then others will have nothing to judge me for.

51. I simply can't forget so I can't forgive.

I know now that holding onto my anger, resentment and past hurts is only holding myself back from happiness, success and achieving my goals. Forgiving is not forgetting. It is simply releasing me from feeling powerless and controlled by past events. It is time to move forward with my own life.

52. Everyone else always gets what they want so something must be wrong with me as I never get what I ask for.

I am worthy of having my deepest wishes fulfilled. There is nothing really wrong with me; I am allowed to be who I am. By believing first in myself and my worth I am entitled to all that I desire.

53. I hate confrontation. I always lose or can't think of things to say.

I will now think of confrontation more as a discussion than a battle of egos and words. By planning what I would like to say first, I will be calmer and more prepared to state my side of the issue. I will also find the perseverance and acceptance to hear what the other party has to say. There really are two sides to every situation and my perception of the original issue may be different from the experience of the other person.

54. There is nothing within me that is worth believing in.

Until I find passion within me, I will continue to avoid knowing myself. My interests towards my own life to make it the best it can be will give me purpose and identity. Then I will have something within me to believe in.

55. I will have nothing left if I let go of my stuff.

By surrounding myself with 'stuff' and 'things' from my past, it keeps me anchored and buried in the past. Although having these things around has made me feel protected, these things also suffocate me and limit my vision of the present or any future waiting for me. Letting them go easily and with joy allows me the freedom to know I have helped someone else, cleaned out unused and broken items and cleared space around me to breathe. It is now OK to begin the journey to free myself and heal and let others help me do so.

56. *If I never show anyone that I am interested in or good at anything I will never have to do something I might fail at.*

By avoiding being involved in my own life, I am simply spinning my wheels and putting my life on hold. I must now get up each day with purpose and conviction that as long as I am working towards a goal or engaged in something I am interested in, then I am alive and vital. Even if I make a mistake, and everyone does from time to time, I will have learned something or met someone new. I am the only one judging myself and it is time to stop.

57. *I always have tomorrow to get things done.*

Even though I realize that whatever I put off until tomorrow will still need to get done, I limit my freedom for new experiences today by delaying my chores and projects until another time. I now decide to take action to work through what I need to do today. It will also give me more freedom to enjoy doing what I would like to do as opposed to only doing what I have to do.

58. *If I forget about what happened and pretend it didn't, I will be free.*

If I deny the pain, hurt, humiliation and other experiences from my past, and shove them away, I realize they just stay stuck somewhere within me, waiting for closure. This limits my freedom to be happy and ultimately my health by keeping these secrets buried. By refusing to address these issues and heal from them, forgive or let them go, I also alter my perception of the world around me. This creates jaded thoughts and opinions and limits my vision and capability for an amazing life. It is time to resolve, heal from, forgive and let go of the past.

59. *True friends don't exist.*

As long as I am not able or refuse to be a friend to myself, I will always reject having others get close. I must remove the barrier of judgment tainted by the past which created my lack of trust in people around me. However, I must first acknowledge my biggest hurdle is in learning to trust myself. To have a true friend I must first be a true friend to myself.

60. *I feel so dead inside. There is nothing that inspires me.*

It is time I allowed myself to notice life around me. Everything I see has the potential to spark deeper thought, images, and new processes. It is time I awakened to my life and allowed myself to feel and see and explore who I really am and what excites me. No one else can make that choice but me to engage in the world around me.

61. *I have given up believing in anything.*

I now will dig deep and find within myself something that I do trust and can count on. No one else can tell me what that is; it is simply time to focus on me. Once I allow myself to take this first step I will find it easier to believe in more about myself. The more I focus and find within me things I feel good about, the easier it will be for me to find my faith and trust in the world around me.

62. *I refuse to be told what to do.*

My stubbornness about being told what to do limits my life experiences and relationships. My perception of being told what to do is really my resistance to change, my history of being controlled by others or the fear of being open to trying something new. I realize that I am here on earth along with others and that collective thinking can offer different perspectives. Listening doesn't mean I need to act on ideas or thoughts presented by others, yet by refusing to at least listen I limit my ability to experience or understand alternative ways to view life. I know what I know, however I will never know what I don't know if I close my mind and ears.

63. *I feel alone and that no one really cares about me.*

It is time I stopped waiting for validation from others and took an interest in my own wellbeing. I am here with a purpose and a life to live and it is up to me to care for and love myself first. As I honour, respect and show myself compassion, it will be easier to relate to others and see that they really do care. I am never alone unless I am the one pushing others away.

64. *I am in a rut and feel there is no way out.*

I have no one else to blame but myself for my boredom and lack of inertia. I now choose to look for things to do and put my energy into getting involved in life and stop my complaining. I am grateful that I can actually make this choice. Once I choose to look up and around me and not just down at my feet, I will see that there can be many options and opportunities for me. There is always a way out...it is simply up to me to find it.

65. *It is always easier to give in to the wishes and plans of others.*

I have a right to my own choices and thoughts as well as having my needs met in life. By offering my suggestions and joining in with the plans of others, they simply become a point of discussion for collective choice. I just may be the one who offers a new perspective or opportunity to enjoy and learn from. Having a voice and asking to do things my way once in a while is validating and not selfish.

66. *If I let myself be vulnerable I will get hurt.*

Being vulnerable is not really about being weak but it is about being open to change and letting myself be aware of the world around me. By allowing me to see and experience the world through child like awe, change and learning can happen. As a confident child fully engages in everything they see, I am ready now to do the same. By doing so I will bring a new awareness for growth through the strength of who I am and what I need and not through self defeating thoughts of weakness or fear.

67. *I don't like looking in the mirror as I never like what I see.*

It is time to own who I am and take stock of where I am as of today. Refusing to look at myself is childlike and won't allow for me to take charge and fix, heal or grow.   I am who I am at this present moment and if I don't look or feel right then only I can take action for change. Not looking doesn't mean others can't see me. It is time to have a good look and see what I need to acknowledge about myself for a better and healthier life going forward.

68. *If I downplay who I am, no one will ever expect much from me.*

I know I have great ideas at times and would love to speak out and join in conversations. By staying in the shadows though, I get overlooked or feel pressured to join in. I know I dislike that feeling so by sharing naturally there will never be any expectation for results from me, except the ones I place upon myself to be real and in the moment.

69. *Nothing will ever change in my life.*

I now realize I am the one holding myself back. By making negative statements of; I can't, I won't, I doubt, I will never, and more, I am the one telling the Universe I am not ready to change. I now watch my words and deliberately make them more life affirming by making statements of what I can do and recognize the things that have worked. This is what attracts more positive things into my life and how change happens. It is up to me to decide to do so.

70. *It is just too difficult to learn anything new.*

I realize I just get in my own way when trying to do something new or different. It is more about my resistance to change and insecurity in how I will be perceived by others than anything else. I now know if I don't make the effort then I will actually never really know whether or not I can learn anything new. I also understand that new things do take time to master and I am not expected to do things perfectly right away.

71. *If I take time for fun, people will think I am slacking off.*

By taking time out, I can recharge my energy and by doing something new or different I am offering myself new life perspectives. My downtime is actually a stress outlet which will help me function better in other areas of my life. Fun is not slacking off; it is a well needed break from the day to day routines.

72. *I push myself to be a good person so no one will see all my faults and weaknesses.*

To keep hiding behind my good will to others simply is a delay in facing up to doing my own healing work. It is up to me to identify areas I consider to be weak and find ways to strengthen myself or grow through them. No one is perfect in all areas and sometimes what I consider to be my faults or weakness really will be my greatest teacher. We were never meant to be perfect just real and vital.

73. *Life is more fun when I knock myself and everyone else off balance.*

Although I find it fun to constantly keep people guessing what I will do next, I know that I do need to find a balance point for stability. From this anchor I will find I am being trusted and respected more and not just accepted as the life of the party. It is also time to see if I am using this behaviour to deflect from being seen to closely.

74. *Doing something just for me makes me a selfish person.*

When I spend the time enjoying something for me it makes me a happier and less stressed individual. I then have more patience and understanding to share with others. I now understand that doing something just for me is not selfish but necessary for my mental, emotional and physical well being.

75. *If I always apologize or say I am sorry people will like me more.*

To say I am sorry when I am not is a lie. To apologize for something I didn't do takes ownership away from the real issue at hand. To infuse my apologetic energy into a situation where it is not needed is interference. I now understand that being genuine when I say I am sorry will have the most meaning.

76. *Life is just too scary for me.*

It is time to face my fears and see what is really holding me back. I know life is meant to be lived and only I can take ownership to push myself to heal and change. Life itself is not what is scary; it is my interpretation due to experiences and programming that has made it so.

77. *If I stay within my comfort zone I will always be safe.*

Always playing it safe keeps me hostage to the results of my past experiences. I know I don't have to go to extremes when trying something new. Small steps towards new things will help me become more confident and trusting in myself. I know there is so much more for me to experience. I can find within me the courage to simply try one thing and when I find comfort and success in that I will know I can do more.

78. *My life is hard enough and I don't want to know about the hardships others face.*

In refusing to get involved and know about the difficulties people face in the world I limit my perspective and ability for compassion. I also refuse to see that my issues may not be as bad as I think they are. Once I open my eyes to what is really going on, my issues in life may seem small and easier to overcome in comparison to others. I may also find a way to assist others through understanding and finding solutions to my own issues.

79. *I can cope better with my life if I look the other way and ignore what is happening around me.*

Until I face the reality of my existence I will be living in an unreal world full of unseen trials. As a result I will be on edge and/or oblivious to the wants and needs of others when I could be the one they need to make a difference. Stuff happens to everyone and to deny or ignore the reality of challenges or results of experiences is a fairy tale existence. This could eventually leave me facing a harsher reality than I could ever imagine, since I never prepared for them or knew they existed.

80. *I have so many regrets, that I am just sad.*

I understand that I cannot change the past and the things that have transpired are now beyond my control. I do have the choice to free myself by facing them now. It is up to me to either seek resolution from the people involved or simply let go of the things I cannot change. Whichever way I choose, forgiving me is the most important and loving thing I can do right now to set myself free.

81. *Nothing anyone can say to me will ever relieve my pain.*

Although I know others may not exactly understand all that I have experienced, they just may be able to offer comfort or insight on how to move past my pain. There are many solutions in life to moving forward and healing and it is up to me to start letting some of them in. I am ready to open my heart and share my hurt and experience so that I may heal. I trust that there are answers that I am ready to hear.

82. *It is just easier to make myself small.*

I know I am here on earth for a reason. To make myself small means others are overlooking my gifts and benefits that I could offer. I now seek help to face my fear of being noticed and as a result my self-esteem and self-worth will blossom. After that, confidence within myself will allow me to find and share the value within me.

83. *Whether I try to love someone or let myself be loved, I always end up getting hurt.*

It is time to stop looking to someone else for love. I know I must first learn to love myself. I must find within myself reasons that make me loveable. Once I know and love myself, I will be able to give and receive unconditional love.

84. *There are so many things I simply hate.*

Using hate as an excuse stops me from being engaged in life. If I truly am uncomfortable with something or someone I could use it as an opportunity to grow and learn more about myself. Once I understand why I am so disturbed I can work through to resolve and neutralize my hate. Hate is an extreme emotion that will hold me hostage.

85. *I don't feel I have any importance in life.*

I have failed to realize that even the smallest kindness is important to someone. The simplest gesture, suggestion or interchange that invites others to also share is important to note. I have more importance than I have been willing to see or own just by being here. I can now find the courage to do things like volunteering and getting involved with others to see the difference my life can make. When I put myself out there freely without expecting compensation is when I truly will feel important.

86. *I resent everything and everyone in my life.*

I see resentment as a trigger for my insecurities when I feel slighted or less than. I can use this as a stepping stone to resolve my feelings and come to terms with the root of this issue. To hold resentment will only hurt me as the ones I love will eventually turn away. I am the only one hanging onto it and I am the only one who can release it.

87. *Unless I feel acknowledged for the things I do, I know they are never appreciated.*

I understand that expecting a reward or consideration for my time and effort when I voluntarily do things for others, eventually makes it awkward for others to receive my help. When I give freely, without strings attached and without expectation, I find I have more to give. My reward is my own internal wellbeing and happiness.

88. *I expect so much from life and yet am never happy.*

My happiness is not dependent upon what I expect out of life. It is about what I invest into my life to create happiness. Expecting something from life is simply sitting waiting for something to happen. And although all our prayers are answered, what can happen isn't necessarily the answer to our happiness. I am ready to remove expectation and change it to participation in my own happiness.

89. *I am so helpless I just give up.*

I understand that giving up, means giving in to defeat. I am not really helpless just lost in what to do next. I know I can reach out for help, and there are many willing to guide me. Some have had similar experiences and I can learn from them. It is time I sought assistance outside of what I know so that I can find solutions to work through this. Asking for help is the first step.

90. *I really want to change but nothing ever works out for me.*

Simply wanting something to happen is a form of inertia. Nothing will ever change without my choice of action. I will now decide what I feel needs to happen and then take the steps to make it so. I know simply wanting change is not enough to create change.

91. *I must be unworthy as anything I have ever hoped for has never happened.*

My faith is strong and I believe to hope is a form of prayer. It is time though to see if I could help myself by setting an intention around the things I hope for. By intending, I will get involved in creating the desired results. This will help me feel more confident and engaged in my own life.

92. *If I tell others what they wish to hear they will leave me alone.*

By telling others what they wish to hear I deny my own right to speak my truth. If they don't like what I have to say that is also OK, as communication is about discussions and interchange of ideas. I will grow, heal and empower myself when I offer my ideas and points of view. I will also find I will be more respected and accepted for the unique individual that I am.

93. *I am tired of being challenged and resent always having to learn.*

I realize that earth is the biggest schoolhouse and the day I stop learning is the day I no longer need to be here. I also understand that when there are many challenges it could be an indication that we may have taken a wrong turn on our path of life. I now will take the time to see why so many challenges are coming my way and find my true path again. Resentment about this will only keep me stuck where I am facing more challenges.

94. *I feel like I always get the wrong end of the stick.*

My life won't change until I change my perspective to focus on the things that are good in my life and not so much on what I think is so wrong. Getting the wrong end of the stick, feeling left out, or never getting my needs met, tells me I am not putting myself out and into situations where people and abundance can be attracted to me. I really am a magnet for all the things I focus on. It is time to focus on what I would like to have happen and not what hasn't or doesn't happen.

95. *If I keep fighting the rules and causing havoc someone might finally notice I exist.*

I understand that whether it is good attention or bad attention it is about the results I desire. Do I simply wish to be noticed for causing a ruckus? Or would I prefer to be respected for the contributions I can make. It is time for me to make a choice as fighting and causing chaos tends to repel the very people I would like to finally pay attention to me.

96. *There is so much missing from my life that I will never be satisfied or peaceful inside.*

When I hide under a blanket statement like this, I absolve myself from personal responsibility laying the blame for my unhappiness on others. Happiness is not a commodity that can be wrapped in a box as a present. To find peace I must look at the parts that I feel are missing and make the effort to either find them or heal from them to create the sense of peace I am looking for.

97. *I constantly must find new friends so I don't have to show anyone the real me.*

Finding new friends all the time although challenging and exciting is exhausting. The value of a lifetime friend brings support and understanding for all the challenges and circumstances we have been through together. To constantly move on and never allow myself to be real, means I am the one judging myself as unworthy. When I finally become real with myself, I will find true friends who will accept all of my quirks, strengths and limitations. I will then be able to celebrate the real me!

98. *If I let this pain and sorrow go away I will start to forget and that is a horrible thing to do.*

Although it is difficult to face sorrow and loss, it is an experience we all have to face at some point. I understand that although I am grieving, once I accept that I cannot change what has happened I will become more peaceful inside. The memories are inside me and unless I choose to let them go they will always be mine to remember. Those that I have loved and lost will always be a part of me. Healing from pain and sorrow might feel like a betrayal but by doing so I will be able to honour their memory more easily.

99. *It's easier to be angry and jealous than to understand how others got what they wished for.*

When I stop comparing myself to others and engage in my own life I will find it easier to attract the things I feel I need. Focusing on emotions such as jealousy and anger will get me nowhere. It is time to decide what I really wish for from life and create a plan to make it so.

100. My life sucks and if I can't help myself I am useless to offer support to someone else.

By offering my help and support to others I will understand that I can make a difference. To compare my life to others or judge my life as worthless is self defeating and takes away from the good I could possibly do. It is time to make the effort and see where it takes me.

101. I pray for patience yet always become more stressed.

I know my prayers are truly answered in the fashion for my greatest good. I also now know that patience is something that grows through experience and acceptance and not something that just happens. Once I relax my expectations for outcomes and face my life circumstances honestly and with intention to succeed, my stress levels will decrease and my patience tolerance levels will grow.

10 *Lessons*

Spiritual Guidance

101 Life Lessons

1. Be grateful. The "attitude of gratitude" multiplies this positive energy returning more to be grateful for.

Showing gratitude and being thankful for the many blessings and achievements you already have will attract more reasons to be grateful into your life. Remember that the energy you project is multiplied and is always returned in kind, whether it is gracious, positive energy or restricted, undermining, and defeated energy. Being ungrateful creates a dense, limiting barrier, as negative energy is thick and heavy with the characteristics of fog, limiting perspective, dulling the senses, and eventually the ability to see opportunities. To always believe you are or have "less than" creates a fight or flight breath, restricting oxygen flow which could eventually result in health issues. Are you able to take a deep relaxed breath right now; then another in a natural relaxed fashion? Another way to think of this is, if you were to awaken tomorrow with only the items that you expressed gratitude for today, what would you have with you? Think about that statement. What would you have today to support you physically, emotionally, mentally, and spiritually? The "attitude of gratitude" is not reserved only for our material possessions, but for all aspects of our lives and on every level. Even if your life seems dismal right now, you still have clothing, or some food, or shelter, or a friend to talk to, or your health, a smile from a stranger, or the ability to breathe, think, and move. We all can find something to be grateful for, however little or insignificant it may seem in the moment. This becomes the seed you sow for a better tomorrow. By focusing on the positive and thus replacing your thoughts on what is wrong, broken, or missing from your life, the Universe will always reward you with more.

2. *Forgive and Accept Self. It is time to stop the self-punishment and recriminations.*

When you have done something that you are not proud of or made mistakes that have negatively impacted yourself or others, the reality is that you did them using the influences, experience, knowledge, or lack thereof that was available in the moment. As they say, hindsight is always 20/20. Yet to hold yourself stuck in self-recrimination denies you the right and freedom to move forward and find happiness. You are entitled to be happy today regardless of past transgressions. It is also possible that if someone else was involved, they have moved on or forgotten the incident. You are the only one wasting energy holding onto the memory. It is a fact that if you choose to continue to hold yourself accountable, you may be the only one suffering, since this doesn't mean that anyone else would choose to suffer along with you. Face up to and own whatever happened. Make amends, resolve, and then make peace with the fact that no one here is perfect. Next, understand that mistakes are simply a way of learning, no matter how big, embarrassing, or irreversible they might seem. Let yourself off the hook so you can open up, receive, and maybe even sing or dance! Lewis Smedes wrote, "To forgive is to set a prisoner free and then discover that the prisoner was you."

3. Forgive others. To forgive does not mean to forget. It is simply empowering to do so and will free you to create a healthier and happier life.

Whether or not a person is willing to say they are sorry to you, find it in your heart to forgive them. When you do not, you allow them to continue to have power or control over your thoughts, actions, and responses to life. In healing, it is important to be clear with your own energy, integrity, and intentions. It is neither healthy nor practical to interfere or hold onto anyone else's energy while waiting for restitution. In any circumstance, no matter how accidental, vile, or intended toward you it may have been, there is always something to be gained or learned. Sometimes the slights or hurts may feel impossible to reconcile. By taking back your power through forgiveness and being the one to let go, you will become stronger and more confident, and your healing will be more complete. Waiting for some form of acknowledgement, apology, or recompense for the devastation you went through constrains your life force energy. This puts your own life on hold. Understand that if someone hurt, abused, or undermined you in any way, it is more about their own insecurities, need to control, or inability to love than your right to be loved. Be clear with your own value. Don't let someone else determine your worth.

4. Stop looking for validation and acceptance from outside. Create your own values, morals, and standards.

Often we seek acknowledgement from outside of our *Self* simply to validate that we exist, seeking to see how others might measure our worth. When we do this, we open ourselves to judgment or expectation of someone else's set of criteria for standards of living and achievement. It is time to go inside yourself, to seek your own true worth, and shine in your own world. The only person you ever have to be good enough for is YOU! Make a list of the things you enjoy or accomplishments you have so far achieved. If it seems limited, think back to when you were a child; remember the things that excited you and that you were able to do easily. Then expand upon them. Have you ever thought of creating a "To Do" or "Bucket" list? Think about where you see yourself in one month, six months, or five years from now. No matter what age you are right now, there are still things that you can accomplish for the simple reason that you choose to!

If you are not working towards your own future, then you are either spinning your wheels and wasting time or helping someone else to create theirs. If you are partnering with someone else in creating their goals, when they are satisfied and the job is complete, where does that leave you? If they become unhappy and change their dream part way through, does that mean you are to blame and now have to invest more time away from your life until they succeed? You were born with certain abilities unique to yourself. You have the right to set your own goals and create your own future. Remember that if you are waiting for someone else to define your worth, you might wait a long time as they may just not have it within them for you.

5. *Let go of the past as it will never change.*

Stop looking back over your shoulder at the things that happened in the past that are beyond fixing or changing. If you could have resolved or made restitution with them, you already would have. If there is the potential to still do so, then what are you waiting for? Otherwise, resign yourself, accept the lesson, and free yourself. What is done is finished and locked into your history. It now becomes a case of "what was" and does not have to impact any longer on "what is." There is no amount of reliving a situation that will change the outcome of anything that has gone before. To hold onto regret or remorse is the same as having your feet stuck in cement, refusing to allow you to move forward into potential, new experiences, and dreams. Understanding the past so we do not repeat mistakes is more than OK, but to hold ourselves stuck, full of guilt, shame, or worse, just keeps us prisoner to that moment and blinded to the potential of our future.

6. *You are worthy of unconditional love, so be open to accepting it!*

It is time to stop believing that anyone, including *Self* is more worthy of love than another is. We do not have to be or think a certain way or accomplish certain things before we can be given love. We are perfect just the way we are no matter what we may have thought, said, or done in the past. Yet most of us tend to dwell on our shortcomings. Believe though, that even in our perceived imperfect state, our ability to be loved does not diminish. Unconditional love given to *Self* or received from others is about accepting our strengths, weaknesses, and being really OK with who we are in that moment. The benefits come when we let love in, in spite of our flaws. Then we can be natural, honest, and open. We were never meant to wait until we were perfect to give or receive love unconditionally. What is the perfect time to allow love into our lives anyway? The answer is right now and just the way we are. Allowing unconditional love into your life will provide the strength, encouragement, and support to bolster your confidence and see you through any situation.

7. *Be a gracious "receiver" not just a determined "giver."*

We have been taught from a very young age that it is more gracious to give than to receive. This is true when we look at the positive reasons for giving. To help, surprise, and occasionally honour a person by making them feel special or supported for a time are genuine reasons to give. "Supported for a time," is an essential phrase, as there is the potential for the recipient to become incapable of relying upon themselves if "only receiving" becomes a standard practice. The imbalance begins when we are giving with an expectation for some form of return. This form of giving sets up a challenge to get recognition. When the giving is unacknowledged, we can become even more determined to give yet again, first, or even faster than before. The unfortunate part of this act is that if giving becomes repetitive, then the expectation switches to the recipient that your generosity will always continue. If you only ever give, no matter how good it feels, it is like making continual withdrawals from your personal energy bank without ever replenishing or investing back. This can eventually leave you exhausted, bitter, energetically bankrupt, or even feeling taken for granted. If you continually give too much, it could also build resentment and be a burden to the receiver, as they know they could never repay in kind. It is time to realize the importance in the act of allowing others to give to you. Letting others make you a cup of tea when they recognize that you have had a difficult day goes miles into replenishing your spirit. Simply allow them the opportunity to be the giver so that you can experience being a gracious receiver. Remove the guilt about not doing everything first and experience the joy you feel when you give by allowing yourself to be given to. This will assist in bringing balance into your life by giving another the opportunity to give to you because it replenishes *Self*, creates a positive energy flow, and strengthens belief in your own self-worth. In fact, why would they wish to give to you if you were not worthy of receiving? It is time to re-evaluate your balance point between giving and receiving.

8. *Mistakes are necessary for learning. Use each one as a growth opportunity.*

Mistakes are an essential part of life. Everyone makes them from time to time. If everything were always perfect, what would inspire us to learn, motivate us to investigate something new, invent a better or different process or product, or produce a brilliant idea? Making mistakes can also define our sense of *Self*. Do we suffer with each one and beat ourselves up? Or, do we rise to the challenge, investigate the error, and get right back on board to create a different ending? If we continued to do everything perfectly, what would we strive for or how would we learn? How boring our lives would be if everything we did was never challenged. Think of the new people that came into your life when you needed to find answers, or the new ideas that flowed because your first idea was rejected. Mistakes are going to occur with or without our permission. That is life and learning. In the movie business, how many re-takes do you think are necessary to perfect a movie from the miss-takes that are made? Then, after watching the finished product, we all laugh and enjoy the out-takes, marveling at the number of times they had to repeat some scenes to get them right. Allow yourself to make peace with not being perfect all the time, and find the value and knowledge gained from this amazing growth opportunity called 'mistake'.

9. *Be personally responsible. Do Not blame, accuse, or hold others accountable for your actions.*

Playing the blame game to deflect attention away from your actions and choices eventually undermines your sense of confidence and self-worth. It is your life after all, so what are you really doing with it? How involved are you with making decisions, taking action, and then owning results? Do you wait until someone else goes first and then regret your lack of initiative, because you really did know how to do something better or faster? On the other hand, do you make a choice and take action, following through to the end? Or, do you try to hold another accountable for your choices and actions? Unfortunately, if you do blame or undermine another and you are in the wrong, it gives them an opportunity for power over you that you might not really desire. Remember that how you treat others offers them the freedom to treat you the same way in return. Respect yourself enough to consider your actions before you take them so that corrections are a minor part of the outcome. If time is limited and immediate action is required, then love and respect yourself enough to be accountable for the results.

There are also times when others would absolutely love for us to take responsibility for something that really isn't ours. This is a deflection away from their responsibility and not ours to own. At still other times, things seem to happen outside of our control.

When this happens, pause, take a step back, then a deep breath, and realize that it isn't always about you. You do not have to be responsible for what is not yours nor what is beyond your control. Accept responsibility for your decisions and the actions that you take. You will never succeed in finding new opportunities for growth and knowledge if you are always looking to deflect your life's responsibilities onto others. Entering into each new day, task, or challenge with the best of integrity, honor, and respect for *Self* and others will create a life of constant positive re-enforcement and happiness.

10. *Trust YOUR inner wisdom. You will never let yourself down.*

It is time to sit still, listen, and allow your inner voice to speak. You do have the answers within you that are needed. Although it may be easier to follow the path of another or to let them dictate a course of events, it can only be through their filters and experiences of what has previously worked for them. Realize that there is no one else who could possibly know you better than you know yourself, for no one has had the same experiences, education, and influences that have led you to where you now are. Yes, we are all energetically connected, yet we each have a purpose or reason for being where we are and doing what we do. If we ask deeply within and are open to accept what we are given, we will always receive an answer. It may not be in words and is more often in feelings or images. The words of a song might come to you or a phrase from a book or poem. The answer might even be in a chance comment overheard while walking past someone in a mall. Whether you find yourself in prayer, meditation, or contemplation, by asking and listening carefully, you will start to hear your own inner wisdom sharing insights, answers and prompts for a more peaceful, trusting existence.

11. *Resolve challenges as they come. Procrastinating only delays the inevitable need for resolution and weighs you down.*

You have nothing to gain by putting your life on hold and waiting for a better time to resolve an issue. Take ownership over your life and intentions as and when they happen, just because they happen. By being current, completing and clarifying issues and challenges when they occur, you invite the potential for new opportunities. If you procrastinate, the energy needed to hold onto the unresolved issues limits any possibility for things new and exciting, until or unless you do. Not resolving life problems as they come along clouds the mind, keeping it occupied with worrying about what to do and playing out scenarios. This isn't wrong as long as you finally pick a path to complete the task. When issues go unresolved for long periods of time, it becomes next to impossible to remember the exact circumstances around the initiating incident. The facts can then become magnified by emotion, confusion, and possibly a need to be right, so what was once a small issue then seems like a mountain to overcome. In addition, to be on task each moment stops the monumental buildup of decisions on what to handle first, and ultimately the exhaustion from being overwhelmed of where to start. It is better to be current than having to come from behind to play catch up.

12. *Be fully present in each moment; neither holding onto regret, nor expectation.*

There is only "now." The past is behind us and nothing can ever change what has already taken place. If you fill this moment with regret, sadness, or any other unresolved emotion for what went on before, then you are holding onto the past, seeking a different outcome. The past is over. Yes, we can learn from it so we don't repeat it. Yet it is and always will be behind us, never to be redone or re-experienced in the same way. Time does move on to today and right now. The future, on the other hand, is ahead of us, full of potential, new opportunities, and challenges, but it is not here yet. If you fill each moment with expectation, you are pushing "now" aside, denying its existence, to get to a time somewhere to be determined. Take a moment to think of the little pleasures and great joys that you might be missing out on, happening right where you stand, if you constantly project yourself ahead. To be fully present in each moment means to be at peace with where you are currently, taking the most from the moment soon to be gone and never experienced again. Regret and expectation are really just excuses to keep you busy so that you can ignore or deny your current feelings. To be fully present in the moment allows for deeper commitment to *Self* because once the moment has passed, a new opportunity is then possible. What you invest in this moment will be what carries you through to build on in the next.

13. *Become grounded. Stand strong on both feet.*

In order to respond and make wise choices in life, it is essential to have two feet on the ground facing forward. We talk of a balanced perspective, or stable outcomes. To be strong and stand on both feet may invite challenge, yes. However, these instances usually lead to greater opportunities and a more exciting existence. If you continue to allow yourself to be pushed around from one extreme to another, it is equivalent to constantly fluctuating back and forth, seeking guidance and wisdom on the run from every direction while trying to find an anchor. Even a swinging pendulum eventually comes to rest. From this stable, centered, and grounded position, you will be able to accomplish your goals, create your dreams, and be on board with your purpose to live a more satisfying life. While the extreme highs and lows of your emotions and choices may stave off boredom, eventually the exhaustion from the momentum will affect your overall health and ability for wise choice. Ultimately, at some point, you will have to find your centre point and get grounded anyway. It is always easier to do something when you choose to do it rather than make it a challenge for the Universe to give you a push.

14. *Be accountable with your words. Speak up when you need to but realize that words, once they leave your lips, cannot be unsaid.*

Consider your words carefully. Find your truth, and speak from that place of confidence and personal authority. Your words will define you and your character as either one who is worthy of respect and further connection or as one who is without integrity. Being accountable with your words does not mean that you have to

125

attack, demean, or defeat another just because you do know better or first. It is about discernment and integrity in the things you say and to those with whom you communicate. There is an appropriate timing for truth, as it truly never needs to be defended. Your motivation for speaking as and when you do is what is being taken into consideration right now. Are you speaking from a point of sharing for a greater good, a need to know information, for the support and encouragement of another, or is it just to hear yourself talk? Your words and the way in which you communicate conveys to others the way in which you wish to be treated. Someone who will stir up gossip to either draw or deflect attention will also use manipulation elsewhere in their life. Speak from truth, integrity, and with purpose so that you will never regret your words. If you have something that needs to be said and is coming from your truth, then build your confidence by speaking and don't hold back. By doing so, you will also find honesty and respect in every other aspect of the world around you.

15. Embrace change; welcome uncertainty as opportunity for new perspectives and understanding.

Change in life is a result of our constant evolution. Change continues long after we die, as our body still has to process change through decomposition. To fear, resent, or try to defeat it by resisting the changes that are bound to challenge us denies your right to new experiences and opportunities, as well as growth in all areas of your life. You are here to learn by being a part of the ebb and flow of energy that is in constant motion around you. To try to stop this course of action for more than an instant would amount to deliberately holding your breath until you pass out. You will eventually start to breathe again, yet you will have lost those precious moments when through change, something amazing could have presented itself. Embrace change and reach for excitement, potential, and opportunity. Resist change and find yourself stuck, bored, and maybe even alone.

16. *Abundance is a state of mind.*

Abundance or lack of it directly relates to a belief system located deep within the subconscious. Entitlement to abundance is not based on anything you have to do. It flows to you as naturally as you believe it can. Start to increase your abundance quotient by focusing your thoughts on the value of your self-worth and also by recognizing and being grateful for what you do already have. When your confidence and self-worth levels expand, they open a runway that continually widens in order to accept limitless amounts of whatever you can dream of from the Universe. If you choose to live within poverty mentality, focusing on what you lack and things you can't yet see, then through this same belief system you will continue to struggle against abundance. This type of focus narrows that same runway and immediately creates limits and barriers for the size, amount, and type of things the Universe may have wanted to place there for you. It doesn't mean that you can never have abundance, it just means you have to be open to the belief that you can. Focus on what you want, removing negative, self-defeating, and limiting beliefs. If you do not have confidence in what you believe you can do or might have, why would it manifest for you since you wouldn't be able to see or acknowledge it? If you received a taste of abundance, you might even think it was mailed to the wrong address, waste it, lose it, or simply give it away. When we remain in an unworthy state, it is hard to accept that we might have the things we wish for. When you shift your focus to believe

127

in and appreciate the abundance all around you as well as within your present existence, the magnetic force this creates will simply bring more abundance directly to you, creating even greater feelings of self-worth.

17. *Faith is the ability to trust in your spiritual connection. Do not just rely on intellect.*

Faith is the ability to trust in a power greater than *Self*, letting go of the tangible and provable. Faith removes the need to be constantly in control so that as we believe we will begin to see. Faith is also about trust. We are so much more than a physical body with a brain. It is about realizing that the spirit within is infinite, with the ability to connect to a bigger source of energy beyond our intellectual capability to understand. The mind is only as powerful as the education, influences, and experiences it has received. While the intellect is powerful, compared to faith, it is limited. Faith is stepping aside, asking, or praying, then being still enough to hear an answer, trusting that our voice is always heard and responded to.

18. *Trust yourself; only then can you trust others.*

Develop trust in *Self* so that you are able to trust others. If you are the one rejecting *Self*, not knowing what is best or right for you, it will be impossible for you to be free to trust another. You may have let yourself down in the past by making mistakes or placing your faith in someone or something that disappointed, hurt, or abused you. To be able to trust others again though, it is necessary to understand that you must first rebuild your own sense of acceptance in *Self*. Trust, in this sense, combines loving *Self*, forgiving *Self*, accepting *Self*, and respecting *Self*. No one is perfect, so work with your strengths and weaknesses, taking back your power to stand strong within *Self*. You could equate regaining self-trust to an exercise program. The more you find ways to trust yourself, the stronger you will be in making the correct life choices. You will also discover that the more you believe and trust *Self*, then as you would do yourself no harm, you will become aware when trust is not earned by another

19. You will get out of life only to the amount you put into it. Stop sitting on the sidelines.

Give yourself permission to live, laugh, enjoy, be happy, and engage in all aspects of life! If you keep waiting for the right time or only when you know an outcome that you can be comfortable with, life will be gone with many special or precious moments wasted. Of course, you also have to be willing to face mistakes and potential failures to know what success really is. This is all part of living and learning. No one is perfect, and if that is your baseline to be involved, then life has a way of pushing you off the sidelines, ready or not. There are no guarantees that life will hand you the brass ring every time. Yet, there is a guarantee that you will always be supported, and through the ebb and flow of opportunity and potential, you will be able to develop the unique individual you came here to be. Through your challenges and experiences, you may also end up being the inspiration that makes a difference for others.

20. Face your fears, for fear is poison to the soul. It also is a challenge to the Universe to help you resolve it.

Fear has been expressed as "False…Evidence…Appearing…Real." Most irrational fears have no basis in logic and end up being debilitating on every level. They can become so instinctual that the reason for them has long since been forgotten. Yet, in really looking at fear, you can see that it is a belief system that has taken on energy. The response to a trigger becomes so strong that we have unconsciously convinced ourselves that we are incapable of overpowering it. This momentary thought, experience, or embarrassment took place in only a fraction of a fraction of the amount of time that we have held onto it, nurturing and investing in its power. It is this power that leaves us without the ability to think or feel logically when confronted. Fear can then be defined as a knee-jerk response that occurs every time we face the trigger that caused us to become fearful in the first place. For fear to continue to exist, all we have to do is continue to react in the same way every time we face the challenge or subject of our fear. Take a moment and look at your biggest fear, but this time try to use logic. Once you identify it, think back to the first moment you felt it. What were you doing at the time? How old were you? Was anyone there to protect, encourage, or support you? Were you embarrassed, hurt, or punished in some way? Was it about a choice you made in trusting or loving? Fears come in all shapes and sizes, and once dissected through logic, you will begin to understand that you actually acted or responded in that moment in the only way you knew how to. It doesn't mean you have to continue to do so. You now have resources to understand what happened at that time and take control over how you choose to react. By facing each fear, understanding why you own and allow its hold over you, you will finally defeat that energy. Removing the perceived limitations from fear assists you in exposing it to the light and removing its poison. The freedom experienced once a fear is resolved is extremely empowering. It is time to expose yours and be free.

21. *Everything you do is an extension and outward expression of who you are inside. Make everything you do be of value.*

We unconsciously have an inner prompt to repeat the same patterns, ending in the same results until or unless we are convinced to change. Having said that, these patterns have us thinking that others will never really know what is going on inside, that we can hide our true feelings or deny our responsibility in a given situation. However, the energy we project out into our life tells a different story. Think of the times that you were unhappy inside and tried to hide it, and yet people just seemed to know how you were feeling. Or other moments when you were so angry and just wanted to be left alone, and everyone wanted to know what was wrong. Conversely, think of the moments you were simply bursting with joy and wished everyone could be as happy as you. Have you ever attended a meeting where one participant was so confused that even in trying to help clarify something, others became confused as well? These are the more obvious visuals of how what we are feeling is easily seen and even experienced along with us by others. It is also how mass consciousness works. One person does or believes in something with such strength that they project a deliberate energetic intention for others to join them. It doesn't matter if it is for good or evil. It just started as a strong energy that attracted others to perpetuate its growth. Again, these examples are tangible proof of our inner manifestation. We also project beliefs and values despite the intention to keep them hidden. Do you tend to procrastinate, cut corners, or shirk responsibility? Or have you ever only told a part or a version of the truth so you could try to deflect attention or responsibility? Maybe you have deliberately limited the amount of energy you put into your relationships or work. Any action we take has repercussions, and if you are holding back or manipulating your involvement in any way, then the result will be that you are limiting the value you place on yourself. Once you are caught in that loop of self limitation and denial of your worth, you actually give others permission to treat you in the same manner. The ultimate undesired result from this form of intentional restriction or manipulation is that you also limit what you are entitled to receive back from the Universe. Face every day offering the best of you with integrity, full on, face forward, and your rewards and experiences will fulfill your wildest hopes and dreams. It is time to value who you are and show it! In addition, remember that as much as what you do is an extension or reflection of whom you are within, others are projecting an extension of themselves as well.

22. *All energy is one energy. Change yourself, and you change the world around you.*

Ghandi wrote: "You must be the change you wish to see in the World." Have you ever witnessed inconsiderate or irrational behaviour against someone or something that simply makes your blood boil? Would you like to see people be more respectful, generous, or caring of each other? Do you believe that there is plenty of abundance in this world for everyone and that deprivation or poverty is unnecessary? Are you stressed and sad when you hear stories of abuse or neglect? How do thoughts of greed and control affect you? These are only a few of the tough issues we read or hear about on a daily basis and yet still only a few of the concerns that surround us. Do you have the ability through time or resources to get involved and make a stand, or are you one who just shakes your head and turns away? If you wish for a better

132

Universe in which to live, then it starts from within you, along with your words and actions. It doesn't have to involve spending money. It begins when you change your attitude and intentions for a better world. If you wish for more kindness, then be kind. If abuse upsets you, then refuse to abuse. Stand up for a person or animal who is suffering. If sadness brings you down, then find a way to make others smile for a while. Simple and pure intention for a fair and wonderful world is a start. Follow that with your actions, and believe change can happen. This plants the seeds for a different outcome. We have more power and control over how we contribute to this world than we realise. You may say that you are only one person amongst a million who suffer. Well, you just may be that one person in a million with a plan or an idea who takes the time to make a difference, creating a better place to live. Check to see what type of energy you are contributing to the world by the actions and reactions of those around you.

23. Resolve, and then share your experiences to help another. Don't hide or deny them.

Earth has been said to be the largest schoolhouse we will ever experience. Every day we are presented with opportunities to know more about ourselves and the world around us by facing challenges of varying degrees and intensities. Some are easy, rewarding, enjoyable, and enlightening. Other experiences stop us in our tracks, creating a feeling inside of being less than capable. These are the ones that when left unresolved undermine our self-worth, leaving us in doubt about who we are or where we fit. Sometimes we prolong the experiences, taking on shame, embarrassment, or even guilt, and keeping them as deep, dark secrets, never believing that we can move past or heal from them.

Since this causes us to isolate ourselves, we start thinking that this has only ever happened to us and that no one could ever understand or even help. It feels overwhelming, and we become too insecure to let another into that moment that changed our life. However, what is done is done. Maybe our choices were not wise in that moment. Maybe we allowed someone to have power over us or were forced to subjugate ourselves to the will of another. So be it. Whatever happened, however we responded, was done based on the influences, information, and environment that we were in at that time. If we had known how to respond differently, we would have, and the outcome would have then been different. It is time to remember that all of this is now in the past and cannot be changed. By facing who we are now, remembering only with the intention to release and heal, we will experience support and encouragement from those around us. Realize that surviving a major trauma, an intense life altering experience of any kind, or even succeeding at something beyond our wildest dreams offers an entirely new perspective of survival and/ or accomplishment in life that could assist others. As a result, you could then be the support you yourself sought, redeeming and strengthening your self-worth. Use the lessons learned to inspire or support someone on their journey, and show them that inner peace and well-being can be achieved out of the chaos of any predicament. After all, you are living proof that it can be done.

24. Be honest. The truth never needs a defense.

Speak about yourself and to others only from the place of honesty. Don't be afraid of your truth or feel that what is valid for you is any less important than what others believe to be true for themselves. Realize that you are entitled to your honest feelings and thoughts. Don't hide from them or put yourself aside to please others. Doing that denies your right to expression and the uniqueness of *Self*. Choose to use discernment in sensitive situations where the harsh truth might hurt or undermine. That doesn't mean to manipulate the truth or delay the reality of it. It simply asks that you speak truthfully in each situation from a place of respect for *Self* and others. You have heard people described as "straight talkers," or others who "sugar coat" the truth. Truth is truth, and no matter how convoluted the path it takes, it does eventually need to be expressed. You will never have to defend honesty, feelings, or actions if your intent is pure, without subtle, dishonest undertones. There is nothing to be gained by innuendo and manipulation. Speak only the truth, and you only have to speak once.

25. It's OK to ask for help. It's not OK to ask others to do that which you are capable of doing.

Asking for help when needed honours not only you but also those who are assisting you. It provides a give-and-take of energy that benefits everyone. After all, you are not on this journey alone, and it does help to ask if you know someone who has survived a similar challenge. By asking for assistance, you are saying that you respect the effort and wisdom they have achieved and are choosing to share in their success. When you do ask for help, it is also wise to remember that not all solutions offered by others are the answers you need. Your challenges are personal, created for your own enlightenment and growth. Sometimes the only way to learn, grow, and see how strong you really are is to find your own answers and solve your own issues. To use others to do that which you are capable of, whether for attention or manipulation, initiates a victim mentality and weakens all involved. To imply that you are incapable of doing something for yourself when you really know you are just being lazy or looking for attention, allows others power over you by creating a debt and a disrespect for the individual that you are capable of being. Stand up and always do the best you can for your own betterment and health. If that isn't working, then and only then seek assistance. This is then a genuine honoring of both souls.

26. *Trust that your prayers are heard and will be answered in a way to achieve the best possible outcome.*

Don't buy into the instant gratification and demands of today. Just because technology seems to be immediate and everywhere, there is still Source, God, or Universal Energy that is greater, more honouring, and more supportive than a machine can ever be. It is a collective energy that, with or without our belief, continues to exist and is always available to support us when we ask. When the power goes out, we flounder without technology and become frightened when the air around us becomes still without the white noise we are so used to. Yet it is in those still, silent moments of hearing only our own heart beat that we can recognize our existence. You can access those silent moments when you still yourself, offering gratitude for what you already have, and then a prayerful request for what you need. Taking time to relinquish control, reflecting, and then asking for assistance from a higher power is an act of empowerment and trust. Knowing that your small, still voice is always heard, and then allowing the answers to come, makes it possible for even better outcomes. We are truly worth more than we will ever know. Let go of a perceived response and simply allow yourself to voice your fears, hurts, needs, and desires through prayer. Be humble and grateful when you practice the act of prayer, then be still, and trust that you have been heard. The answers will come.

27. *Be humble. Humility opens more doors than aggression.*

To push something or someone in life creates an instant response to re-balance that energetic motion by being instantly pushed back. Why set something in motion that subsequently will have to be resolved or brought to rest? To resist the urge of your ego to demonstrate your strength or authority over a situation or individual shows levels of confidence, self-worth, and honoring within. To be humble does not mean to sit back and allow others to walk over you. To be humble in this reference is to be modest and respectful of the rights and beliefs of others. It is about knowing how to allow others their moment while giving yourself permission to stand strong in your own beliefs when needed.

Be a support for others when asked. Ask for support when you are in need. Do this without comparison, judgment, or even comment. Being humble is not about denying *Self*, just being secure and balanced enough within to allow others the same respect for wherever they find themselves on their path.

28. *We are all equal; valued not more or less from one to another.*

We all have a purpose, gift, talent, or a passion deep within that makes us unique and special in this world. It does not make us better or worse, greater or less than our friend, neighbor, family member, boss, or even the stranger on the corner. To compare yourself to others sets limits and unrealistic expectations around your ability to create, succeed, and grow in life. You can be an inspiration to someone or be inspired by another. However, if your focus is outward, you will be missing out on the true essence of who you are. If we simply focus on being the best we can be and bring out the qualities of our true nature, we will each see how we fit together like a puzzle. Each piece will be of equal importance without greater or lesser impact due to its position in the completed picture.

29. *Give back. Re-invest and share your blessings.*

Although we are individually unique and independent, we were never meant to live in isolation. We are all part of a collective energy. To be a part of it requires a constant ebb and flow, a give and take of the very essence of who we are. In the much bigger picture, we are truly blessed in life no matter where we find ourselves. No matter how little or great, there is always something from our list of blessings that we might own, create, or offer that simply might make the difference between feast and famine to another. Whether we give time, comfort, ideas, money, or support, it is essential to share a part of who we are. If you honor others and share, then life has a way of multiplying your blessings in return. It is simply a natural fact that whatever you give in life is returned ten-fold. However, if you block yourself off and hold on too tight, you create a barrier between you and the world and will one day wonder why you are so alone.

30. *Break through resistance. Whatever you resist in life will only persist until you do.*

Whatever you resist in life will continue to persist until you find a way to achieve balance over it. Break down the wall that you are stuck behind by identifying it, facing the emotions that put it there, and/or resolving the issues that created it. You are strong, with more power than you could ever believe. Once you decide to overcome your resistance to whatever is holding you hostage, you will find that you have more support, opportunities, and happiness than you thought possible. Resistance can be equated to the excuses behind which we hide. In reality, resistance is just thick energy stuck in place, creating a barrier to movement and progress. It is also a magnet attracting to you more of the same unresolved issues. The Universe will attempt to help you identify your resistance so that you can find a way for resolution. Poke a hole in your barriers, seek to crumble the resistances between what you wish for and where you now find yourself, and get your life moving again.

31. *Allow inner peace. It is always a choice of how you handle stress and challenge.*

Stress is healthy when it motivates you to do something positive. Challenge is part of life and learning and is essential to self-discovery. By allowing the challenges of our day-to-day life to go unresolved, we create within us a magnet that simply attracts more of the same. Stress then builds and builds until we find ourselves ill or wanting to hide for a while. Sometimes we feel like giving up and starting over. The solution could be right before us, but we can't see it because we are blinded by our exhaustion. When you find yourself taking many sick days because you need a time out to de-stress, think of how much more rewarding it would be to take a well day for a change. Take time out to meditate or pray to find that place of inner peace and acceptance inside you. Be still and quiet; spend time listening to the wind, the sound of your own breath, or even your subtle inner voice. By doing so, you will have more strength and understanding to cope with the stresses in your life. Your health will improve, and you will find empowerment and connection within to a much larger world.

32. *Honour your family, friends, and acquaintances. Show others you care while they are still in your life.*

Do not take for granted the love and support you are given. Unconditional love and acceptance are neither rites of passage nor anything you can demand. They are gifts given freely by those who really care. While you still can, speak of how you feel, be clear, and allow the vulnerability of connectedness to show. We are not isolated beings removed from the need for personal contact or commitment. Keep in touch with family, friends, and those who have been important to you. Let them know how much you appreciate the difference they made in your life. Unconditional love is a gift of honoring, acceptance, connection, and forgiveness. We are all here on a journey. It is what you do and express along the way to those who deserve it that makes living worthwhile.

33. *Resolve and release Shame and Guilt. These come from the past and stay until you let them go.*

Shame and guilt are the leftover results of unresolved issues from circumstances that continue to replay repeatedly in the mind. You have choice as to how long you own, hide behind, and punish yourself with them. In some instances, they are feelings that others might like us to own, which stops us from progressing. If someone wearing a protected body suit, gloves, and oxygen mask tried to hand you a piece of putrefying, pus-coated, stinking meat when you walked unprotected through a doorway, would you simply accept it? Doing something to deliberately feel guilty or intentionally to bring shame or embarrassment seems like irrational behaviour, defying logic. Why would you choose to take them on and own them? While the impact from these moments seems to stay with us forever, they will only last as long as it takes to make the choice to resolve, understand what happened, and wash our hands of them.

Find a way to make peace within yourself, maybe through prayer, talking to others, or facing the choices made at the time. To look back and judge yourself with your current knowledge and experience is unfair to you. In the moment that shame or guilt was created, it was done with the influences and knowledge you had at the time. Remember if there are people who would love to heap guilt on you or make you feel ashamed, then that is their issue. You do not have to accept anything from anyone that you do not choose to own. You are wiser now, a different individual; let go of the things you cannot change. Make peace with past shortcomings.

34. *Face challenges with courage. They are never bigger than your ability to triumph over them.*

We all have challenges, and as we face them, we learn many things about ourselves and life. They help us develop skills and tools to better ourselves or to use and share with others. If we run from or ignore them, we will find that the challenges do not stop. They just seem to get harder, becoming more persistent as they continue to pursue us. Then we are stuck in the avoidance loop of life, with increasing issues of insecurity, ill health, and imbalance, grasping at quick solutions that will not last. As each challenge presents itself, realize that on a deeper, subconscious level, there is something that you need to understand. It could be an experience to inspire growth, or to force us to look at our shortcomings so we can strengthen our faith in our *Self* or others. Every challenge, once resolved, can increase feelings of self-worth and confidence. Although some of our circumstances in life seem insurmountable in the moment, draw on your inner resolve to never let yourself down. Stand your ground and face each challenge as it comes for the experience of learning and growth provided. If you dig deep inside, you will find that you have exactly the strength, courage, and support you need to break it down and then climb over it. It will never actually be bigger than your ability to triumph over.

35. *Stop waiting for someone to rescue you. You are stronger than you believe.*

When our Ego (survival indicator of flight, freeze, or fight) is out of balance, it either sets up a pendulum-like action where being either a victim on one end or a bully on the other seems the only way to survive. These are the extremes of insecurity, anchored into basic survival, without any possibility to move into thriving and flourishing. If you continually wait to be rescued, you are denying your own right to define your existence. This turns your ability to survive and the manner in which you are to do so, over to the control and beliefs of someone else. This does not include the times when you actually do need assistance. We all will experience those. This refers to the conscious choice to sit back, waiting for others to come to your aid. Please know that you came to Earth already owning the power within to achieve anything you set as an intention. To wait for someone else to do the things great or small, denying what you really are capable of doing yourself, simply keeps you a victim. Like a muscle, if you don't choose to exercise your ability to control your own destiny, then you just get weaker, and will eventually have no choice but to depend on others.

36. *Take charge over YOUR life, not someone else's.*

Making yourself the centre of your own world is not an act of selfishness. Nurturing yourself and exploring your interests and passions expands and strengthens your energy field, making you a more valued person. It is equated with making an investment into *Self*, so you have more to offer when asked. It is the only way for you to discover who you really are, and then contribute to the world. To take charge over someone else's existence denies their right for setting and achieving their own goals and intentions in their own way. Because of your experiences, belief systems, and abilities, to intentionally dominate another allows them to only see life through the filters you have created. Partnering and assisting when and only if asked enhances life and strengthens everyone.

37. *Get motivated. Set achievable goals.*

You will never accomplish anything without an agenda or purpose. What do you secretly desire: money, better health, stronger relationships, a vacation, or more? How would your world be different if you actually achieved whatever you set out to do? Unless you identify a reason to get moving, you will never develop the energy needed for change, and you will succeed in only weakening yourself further. Think of what needs to happen for you to move out of the rut that you exist in. Sit down now and commit to paper your wildest dream or goal. Then on the same paper, draw the picture of a ladder resting along the inside wall of a deep hole. In order for you to achieve anything, you have to go up the ladder to get out of the dark void of inactivity. Define each rung of the ladder as a step that must be finished in order to get to the goal at the top. Hold the image in your mind and, with the intention of reaching the top of the ladder, set a date to begin working through the first step. Feel the excitement of success as you begin to climb out of the hole! By accomplishing each small achievable step on the ladder, you are exercising the energy of change, increasing the potential for synchronicities to support you. If you do this, you will see just how powerful you truly are.

38. *Value time spent with Self as sacred. Get in touch with the deeper, connected part of you.*

There is a difference between being alone and being lonely. Loneliness stems from unresolved issues and insecurity in the ego. It is the process of searching to define the *Self* by driving us outward to find that someone or something to make us feel complete. Once we are with that special person, place, or thing our loneliness may disappear for a while, only to return when we need validation of our worth again. Being alone, when used in a constructive way, is a sacred time, invaluable to rebalancing and harmonizing your personal existence, energy, and worth in this world. Consider it a self-help or discovery tool, offering an opportunity to recharge your true inner *Self*. To be alone intentionally, without outside interference, is vital for setting goals, evaluating your achievements, and listening to your own wisdom. To resolve the lonely feeling, one has to go out and join others, which creates opportunities to gain different perspectives. Being alone helps us to learn from the deeper, more spiritual, and wiser part of *Self*. Plan to spend time being alone, and if possible, make it into a routine. By being alone, you will discover your meaning or purpose in this life. If you cannot stand to be alone with yourself, how would you expect to fit in elsewhere? Treat time spent alone as sacred. Value yourself as an individual; delve into what makes you strong or weak, set goals to open up to change, and release stuck or pent-up emotions. As you spend this time getting to know your sacred *Self*, you will carry a new confidence into the world around you making it a better place for everyone.

39. Be willing to learn, or you will stop achieving.

There is a saying that to stop learning is to die. Challenge yourself to explore the things you simply do not yet know. Try listening to a different music genre or read a different style of book. Ask questions, or join groups that offer a differing perspective on your routines in life. Try something totally outside of your comfort zone. Don't feel intimidated or "less than" if there is something you just don't know. We are all students. When we have the answers, we become the teachers. Being open to learn brings its own strengths and rewards for accomplishments, with the added benefit of new discoveries and interests. You might even learn that you have talents, skills, and interests never before identified. To let the *Self* be as a child seeing and sensing new and different things for the first time opens one to new opportunities and a greater potential for an amazing life. Simply give yourself permission to say, "I don't know, but I am ready to learn."

40. Listen with an open mind and heart.

Do not pre-judge yourself or others when there is an opportunity to share ideas, thoughts, or experiences. Resist jumping to conclusions, rushing to interpret, or interrupting to share an even bigger or (in your opinion) better story. When someone is speaking, let this moment be about them, and really listen to what they have to say. The ability to listen is actually a gift of healing. Just to be there for someone when they need to express themselves without trying to change, fix, or judge their words allows a release of energy that builds self-worth for both parties. It has been said that this is the reason why we have two ears and only one mouth. Remember that if you cannot be silent and simply listen, you are showing a distinct lack of respect, acceptance, and patience. Allow yourself to develop the art of listening without pre-determining an outcome. You will know when it is time to contribute and add to the conversation. If you have actually taken the time to listen with an open heart and mind, then your input will be of value and welcomed. This provides the opportunity to explore options, solutions and creative ideas through shared discussion. Being open and ready to listen allows for freedom of expression, adventure, greater potential for understanding, and an appreciation for something new.

41. *Radiate love and respect for Self and others in all ways and at all times.*

Treat others with the same care and consideration that you yourself would like to be treated. To denigrate or disrespect another allows and actually gives permission for the same treatment to be heaped back upon you. When you have respect for yourself, you will emit a constant, positive, loving flow of respectful energy, from yourself and to others. Should you encounter someone of disrespecting intentions, your energy will not be diminished as you will simply not allow yourself to be undermined or brought to the lower level of negative energy. Be clear in the manner in which you would like to interact with others and radiate that love and respect at all times.

42. *Remove arrogance. It is the spark that ignites violence. Become Assertive, and you will find balance in life.*

Do you really believe you have more importance than another does, or are you just looking for a fight? Arrogance sets a challenge to those around you to see if you can be bested and creates a wall that keeps others away. It is a sign of insecurity or possible self-loathing in that you aren't happy with who you are and where you find yourself. It is an inner prompt that drives you to attack first so you will always win or be right. From this perspective, arrogance will never create honest, lasting relationships. Examine what it is you are wishing to hide by using this boastful, aggressive, belligerent wall of arrogance. Take yourself off your self-entitled pedestal to make peace within before someone finds your weakness and knocks you down.

On the other hand, do you feel you lack in importance in aspects of your life? Do you always give in, feeling inferior to others? Assertiveness rather than arrogance speaks to feelings of self-worth and self-respect. To be assertive allows for respectful interactions and inspires healthy relationships through which everyone involved benefits. We all belong in this world and are equal in value and recognition. We all have things to offer of differing intentions and interests. Remove the defense of arrogance and control while continuing to believe in your own self-worth and you will find acceptance, better relationships, and the inner peace and balance that is essential to your well-being.

43. *Respect the input from others, but live by your own guidance.*

Everyone has an opinion to offer, based on their life experiences, belief systems, and influences. Some will share their opinions without even being asked. These may have no bearing whatsoever to help or hinder your situation. Allowing yourself to be pressured to follow a path that is uncomfortable or deviates from your original intention takes you off course from your true purpose. Eventually, you will have to find your way back. To accept this input as a form of learning, communication and expression, and to allow others to have their moment does not obligate you to follow their advice. You alone have the ability to find your own answers based on your own wisdom and perceptions. You may agree or disagree with others. Look for suggestions, direction, and/ or support, but ultimately, it is your life, and it is your choice as to what needs to happen for your greatest good.

44. *Have patience with yourself. There is a reason to trust in a higher purpose without despair and self-recrimination.*

We are not here to be perfect all the time. We are here to learn. It is Ok to be wrong, make a mistake, be late once in a while, disappoint a friend, or simply take time out. Take the time to process why these things happened, and then change the pattern. No matter the occurrence, it is time to stop being so hard on yourself. Are you gaining anything by being self-critical and judgmental? Does this lack of patience with your shortcomings inspire you to seek help, answers, or opportunities for change, or is it holding you hostage to your emotions and feelings of low self-worth and self-esteem? We all have times of being insecure and feeling less important than others. Use those moments to understand the learning process, admit you just don't know, then get up and do something about it. You will find that there is always a reason why events and our reactions to them occur. Part of the time, it is for us to gain a deeper understanding about ourselves and life in general. Other times, our actions may be the catalyst for change in others. There is always the opportunity for growth to be gained from every experience. Instead of beating yourself up over your frustrations and trials, accept where you are, and be patient. After that, trust that if you ask for guidance and support, it will be given.

45. *Find balance in all areas of your life. Single-focused obsession eventually weakens you.*

Each of us is a multi-faceted being. There is time to work, to play, to be serious, to reflect, to rejoice, as well as time for anything else we could think of to enhance our existence. We are designed to absorb knowledge and be healthy through multiple avenues of experiences. To solely focus our time on one or two aspects of life, such as relationship, fitness, finance, or work, denies a balance that eventually takes a toll on mental well-being and physical health. Draw a circle, and write headings around the outside edge such as work, relationship, fitness, nutrition, finance, social life, continuing education, family, stress outlets, creativity, and spiritual or religious time. These are just suggestions, so feel free to list the headings of importance to you. With a pencil, divide the circle into sections to show the amount of time and energy you invest out of your day or week under each heading. Check to see how balanced your life actually is. Which headings take the most of your time? Which ones have you been ignoring? Are you well rounded with lots of outlets and interests, creating multiple opportunities for excitement and adventure? Or have you created a single-focused, obsessive life? Do not wait to look back only to wish you had enjoyed and experienced more out of your life. The time has come for you to re-balance your energy, your time, and ultimately your total well-being.

46. *Respect and honour your physical self. It is literally the temple for your soul.*

When was the last time you thought about the type and amount of food you are eating, or the amount of fresh air and exercise you are getting? Have you had a medical check-up lately to see if there are any hidden problems? Do you rest or take time out to de-stress when you need to? The physical body is like a suitcase that houses your spirit or soul. It is constantly on the move, going from one place to another. As the seams, fabric, and zippers of a suitcase thin out, become weak or stressed, and need repair, the physical body will also fall apart if left without attention. To be proactive in treating the physical body with respect and love, constant nurturing and tune-ups will create a healthier, happier, longer lifetime to achieve your dreams and goals.

47. *Flexibility – learn how to relax your need for control.*

There are times in life when order and control are important. These moments inspire us to stand up for ourselves and speak our truth. There are other times, however, when release of that control allows for new perspective and unexpected opportunity. Lighten your hold over expected and predictable outcomes. Engage in spontaneous moments when called for and be flexible to change. There is so much more to life than being a rigid brick wall that will eventually crack with time and strain. Align yourself with the vision of a tree. A tree is secure through its roots into the ground, with its branches spread high and wide out to the fresh air and sky, and its trunk solid but flexible enough to bend and not snap in the wind.

48. *Never hold yourself back from your dreams; believe you are here to make a difference*

It is important to explore your options in life and to follow your dreams. Do you dream? Do you have those moments of freedom where there are no limits or restrictions to your wishes or desires? When did you last lose yourself in a daydream, doodle with coloured pencils, or write down a creative fantasy? Have you ever been inspired by a song or poem to think outside of or beyond your current reality? Without pausing long enough to dream, inventions would never come to life. Without flights of fancy and creative thinking, new opportunities or methods for problem solving would never happen. If you aren't creating and working towards fulfilling your own dreams and goals, check to see if you are invested in creating someone else's. While dreaming is necessary, implementing or acting upon the dream is equally as important. Resisting the urge to dream or deliberately blocking your own creative process will not support a happy, fulfilling existence. Start with an idea, make it bigger, and finally take it outside of the world of dreams and into reality. You never know what will happen next, because if you can dream it, you can find a way to make it happen. Go for it!

49. *Telling lies for any reason, even to yourself, will always bring you down to a lower, less healthy vibration.*

We are all guilty from time to time of telling ourselves or others little white lies. Sometimes we will even tell others what we think they want to hear, altering the truth to fit a desired result. At times, a lie is used to deflect personal involvement or responsibility. Sometimes, only part of a truth is all that is spoken. While we may think it is OK in the moment, lies or half-truths accumulate and build negative energy that eventually seeks balance. Lies of any sort eventually need to be defended. Once begun, they start a convoluted web of confusion. Truth is the opposite. If something is true, it is absolute, without question or need for defense. Think about your words and speak from the place of truth, not to deliberately hurt or offend, but simply to be honest. The bigger consequence of little white lies or part-truths always ends in disrespect or lack of trust for you and your word.

50. Trust in a power higher than Self – Source, Universe, God – the energy that is "all that is."

When you have nowhere else to go or no one else to turn to, what are your options? There is a power greater than all of us, just waiting to be acknowledged and asked to help. This power comes with a feeling of limitless unconditional love and support and is available for everyone. All that is required is trust, being humble, open to suggestion and being grateful for whatever is shown to you or comes your way. Just ask and then allow. What do you have to lose?

51. *Trust in the Act of Forgiveness. When others are willing to release you, just accept and let go.*

Forgiving *Self* and forgiving others are gracious and generous acts of humility, understanding, and empowerment. Accepting forgiveness from others for issues or acts we created requires belief in the Act of Forgiveness. If others are willing to let you off the hook for wrong doing or hurtful misdeeds, why hold onto that imbalance of energy to continue to punish yourself? If they no longer hold you accountable, then you no longer need to bind yourself to them. Allow this simple act of love, respect, and courage to set you both free. Forgiveness is not forgetting, it is simply releasing the hold and setting all parties free to move on with their lives.

52. *Share in and allow for the happiness and successes of others.*

Life is not always a competition, where if another gets promoted or wins a lottery, it means you lose. The success of someone else is not a dispersion cast against you as a failure. Everyone is entitled to their time to shine. Allow yourself to honour and respect their achievements, to support them, and to share in their happiness. The easier it becomes for you to do this, the more happiness and success you will attract into your own life. Also, do not take offense if there is a time when you feel a sense of reluctance from others to share in your achievements and joy. That is simply a reflection of their need for comparison or competition. When it is your turn for praise or acknowledgment, there will be many more to celebrate and share it all with you.

53. *It is time to confront an issue that you have been avoiding.*

Confrontation for most is a very difficult concept. Yet if you change the words to that of having a discussion and speaking your truth from the depth of your soul, the idea of confronting the issue changes to one of owning your self-worth and not that of a fight. Whether the issue lies within as something to own up to and face or with another, the process to success is the same. Take time to sit still with paper and pen. First write down what your objective is once this issue is resolved. This could be to pay off a debt, or suggest to a friend it is time they found and acted on their own answers. Maybe it is to resolve an argument and clear the air to stop a pattern that keeps repeating. Whatever the reason may be, be clear as to why facing this issue is now necessary. How will your life be different? Will you feel a sense of closure or freedom from worry? Maybe you are the one who needs to apologize. The reason doesn't matter as long as the path is towards the truth of a situation which then allows for the freedom that comes from letting go. Next, be honest and write down how you got into this predicament. Were you shocked into silence and then others moved on leaving you undecided on what to do in the moment? Did you fail to speak up when you had the opportunity because you just didn't know what to say? Did you deny your feelings to save the feelings of someone else, only to have them move on without feeling any sense of responsibility for the encounter? Did you cut someone off and fail or refuse to hear all sides of the situation? There are so many reasons why we withdraw, leaving issues unresolved. Once you realize why you need closure and how you got into the predicament, organize the statements you wish to say. This doesn't matter if you are giving yourself a pep

155

talk, finding the words needed to apologize or needing to speak to a person of authority. If you come from a place of truth, with logic for what you feel happened and what you feel needs to be done to resolve the issue, you open the door for discussion and the perspective from others that were involved. Practice out loud and in front of a mirror if possible until you feel the truth deep within your soul. You will then find the courage to speak your truth and receive closure over any issue. Believe that a confrontation can become a discussion if you choose it to be so.

54. *Believe in yourself.*

Something interesting happens when you believe in yourself. Like a magnet, you will attract others that also believe in you. You will also become more aware of where your support and encouragement really are and where or through whom it is not. We are all entitled to a life filled with happiness and success. By believing in yourself and knowing that you are worthy of this is half of the challenge to receiving it. When you really get to know, appreciate and accept yourself, there is a confidence that naturally emanates and surrounds you. This sends out a strong, peaceful and non-judgmental vibration that encourages others to find their own beliefs about themselves. Believing in self begins when you identify your strengths and shortcomings and accept and make peace with them. We can always improve ourselves of course. Yet, in life sometimes we are simply stuck with the things we cannot change. Work with the ones that you can such as your interests, passions, and strengths and build them into an unshakeable foundation. By believing, you can make the effort to take the steps to be the best that you can be and worthy of your own belief in *Self.*

Once you do, miracles can happen when some of those things that you felt might not change just simply do.

55. *It is time to clear the clutter.*

Think about the things you are holding onto. Look into your corners and pull out the drawers where you have been stashing and storing things for years. Every object as well as having a memory attached also has an energy that may be holding you hostage to an event or emotion long past it's effective, hurtful or supportive due date. Pick up each item and ask yourself what the benefit is to keeping it. Start with one corner or drawer of one room. Have 3 receptacles ready when you do this. One is for absolute garbage, the next for recycle because if it no longer serves a purpose for you it certainly might offer pleasure or assistance to someone else and the last would be for things you simply wish to hold onto. Once you have cleared one spot, give yourself a hug before moving onto another. Set yourself a goal of maybe clearing a certain number of drawers or closets before rewarding yourself with a break of some sort. Then go back and feel the shift in energy from that area. If there is time, tackle another set of drawers or boxes, reward yourself and later go back and feel that new shift. The momentum for change builds once the energy is shifted due to the sense of freedom sorting out the clutter brings. There is also the feeling of helping others when you give the useful things away that you no longer need. Realize that the stagnant energies from things of the past may also hold a chaotic energy once stirred up. Healing, closure and the inner peace that comes from moving it out though, will outweigh the perceived trauma of letting it all go. Time does move on, things from the past are always just things from the past.

As you clear your clutter decide what from the past really does have value and let go of what simply does not.

56. *Are you betraying yourself?*

When was the last time you gave yourself a hug or a pat on the back? When asked "how are you today?", do you immediately answer "good or fine" when you know you are anything but? Do you praise or undermine your self-worth? Are you even aware of the value you project from yourself that allows others to judge you by? When was the last time you graciously accepted acknowledgement of a job well done. Are you afraid to shine and stand in the truth of who you really are? One of the most difficult challenges is to accept ourselves as we are and to love ourselves anyway. We all make mistakes, disappoint or hurt ourselves and others on occasion. It happens because we are here to learn. Yet, when self-talk is constantly about not being good enough, smart, funny, healthy, educated, or other self-defeating statements, we hold ourselves hostage and limit our abilities to engage in activities that excite and satisfy. When did you last recognize your personal worth? Are you making excuses, lying, or betraying your faith in yourself, your abilities or even your desire to face life in a different way? It is time to be honest about you. This starts with acknowledging that you do have value and then finding ways to increase your own worth.

57. *It is never too early to put your house and affairs in order.*

Where are your most important documents right now? Are your bills paid and up to date? Do you have a plan for clearing credit card debt or bank loans? Have you prepared financially for your future? Has any thought been given to who might be able to offer help if you were in need? Who would be able to look after your children or partner you if you had to go to hospital? If something were to happen to you in the next moment could someone step in and help? Are your bill statements, tax information, financial papers, health insurance or other legal documents, end of life thoughts and notations organized in one area? Do you have any idea of your total financial worth? Have you documented names of beneficiaries, Powers of Attorney for both medical and financial assistance or created a Will? Have you made promises in jest to some family members or friends of passing on items when you are through with them? None of us can really predict when or if something might happen. You are simply being asked in this moment to recognize that scattered and incomplete paper work makes it difficult for anyone to assist us when or even if that time comes. Organize now and then relax and enjoy living.

58. *It is time to make peace with your past.*

Are you hiding a deep painful secret inside? Are there things from the past you would have said to someone that hurt, abused, disillusioned, abandoned or undermined you in any way that you never got the chance to say? Are there people you would like to ask forgiveness from that you feel you have hurt? It doesn't matter if the recipient(s) are still living or not, energy from a dark place that is contained and buried eventually needs to be expressed or will cause issues with your well being. You are being asked to finally allow closure and healing by expressing your thoughts, hurts, pain, anger, and anything that has never been totally expressed by putting this in a letter. *Sending it is not the issue, expressing it is.* Take the time to release all the pent up negative and dark feelings you have been holding onto by writing or typing them to the specific person or event to get them out of your system and out of hiding. Addressing these issues will finally allow the hurt to be replaced by healthy and fresh energy. There is no need to rush this process so let it unfold over a day or more. Record some thoughts and walk away and then return and make additional changes. There are no time restrictions to this form of healing. Make peace within yourself by placing all that has disturbed you both towards and/or from others out into the open and on paper. Then for closure, after re-reading and making sure all that needed to be said at this time is in writing, crumple the paper, and either burn it, rip it up and flush it away, or smear it all and bury it. Once that is done remember to breathe deeply and give yourself a huge hug. You will now have a different outlook on life. When the time is right you can revisit and go through this process again with a different issue. You are being asked to feel the freedom that life offers when you finally express and release the hidden, buried and possibly shameful pain from the past.

59. *What type of friend or partner are you?*

How do you relate to others? Do you love a good discussion where there is freedom to state opposing viewpoints? Do you try to fill a void or need in someone's life? Can you respect the differences between people or are you more comfortable when everyone is on the same page thinking and doing the same things? Do you, your partner or any of your friends challenge each other to grow, learn and explore? You are being asked to look at yourself as an individual and see what you offer when relating. Have you explored your own strengths and shortcomings? Be mindful of another's life and choices and offer help only when asked. Don't try to solve their problems because your answers are only based on what has worked for you and no two situations are ever the same. It is far more empowering to ask what they feel needs to happen next or what they have already tried than to offer your answers and solutions. Always respect the privacy of a person's life, have fun and be supportive but not demanding of recompense because you feel it is now your turn to be helped. A true friend or partner helps when asked, says no if they can't and doesn't interfere or meddle. There is no need to see if the suggestions made are being followed. However, to be a true friend or partner means first being a friend to you! Are you happy on your own? Do you do your best to never let yourself down? When you offer unconditional love and support first to yourself you will automatically have the ability to remain impartial and non-judgemental towards others. You will also receive the same respect from others when you find yourself in need. Be the friend or partner to yourself that you would like to partner with.

60. *Have you been creative this week?*

We have within each of us a need to let loose now and again; to let our hair down so to speak, and go out and walk in nature. Once you open up you may have an urge to try to paint a picture or visit an art gallery, make something from nothing, bring an idea into reality or find and experience new recipes or foods. Have you ever felt a desire to learn to play an instrument or listen to different genres of music, and as they say...dance like no one is watching? Daily pressures of life, bills, family needs, health concerns and planning for the future plus other situations and challenges that we accept as inevitable take our time and focus. However, if we never explore that creative element inside us all the pressure will get so demanding and extreme that we may eventually crack with the strain. This creative side is our pressure cooker valve. Once we invest some time to routinely explore our interests in some fashion we release stress, anxiety and depression or other of the darker more inhibiting emotions for clearer thought and practical assessment of our lives. Take the time right now and every week to get creative, explore the fun side of life, accomplish something new and different and find peace within yourself.

61. *What do you believe?*

Do you believe in a Supreme Being or power that is greater than all of us combined? Or, do you believe in the precision of science, of cause and effect and require proof and validation? Do you believe in the goodness of human nature or has life been too harsh for you to reconcile that thought? Maybe you were raised to believe that life is always a struggle and success is for the other person. You could also have been raised to believe that you are entitled to everything you want and that everything should come easily when you ask for it. Whatever it is you choose to believe in is your choice. However, understand that this belief becomes the building block for creating your reality. As what you believe always dictates the type of action you take or attitude you have toward life, then your beliefs can be the determining factor in achieving your goals. Being either too pessimistic or overly optimistic may be holding you hostage to creating the dreams you desire. Find the balance that brings potential and opportunity. Ultimately you are being asked to believe in the value of you. Once you do you will find doors opening, opportunities presenting themselves, and the support to achieve any goal you set being offered if you choose to accept it.

62. *What inner prompt have you been ignoring?*

We all have a small, still but clear voice within that is asking us to pay attention to something. It is the prompt that wakes us up when the alarm doesn't go off so we aren't late for work. Or stops us before leaving the house to make us think of something we are forgetting. This voice also prompts us to make a doctor's appointment or call someone we haven't heard from for a while. We might even hear it when we cheat on our diet taking too much food or drink. However, this prompt can also guide us to look for a new job, or alert us to danger causing us to cross a street and walk down the other side when our physical eyes haven't seen anything. Maybe your prompt is saying to get off the couch or chair and move, or find your camera and go for a walk in nature. By ignoring this prompt from within you are missing out on your own personal support system and guide to keeping you safe, healthy and engaged in life. What is your prompt telling you right now?

63. *What are you searching for?*

Do you feel there is something missing from your life? Have you identified it as a vague feeling of discontent or is it like a large beacon of light pointing out a void or deficit? Take the time to acknowledge that life might just be better once you identify and resolve what is missing. Searching without direction or knowledge of what you need is wasted time and energy. Sit down now and ask yourself what it is that you have lost or is missing from your life. What are you really searching for and is it something that is essential to a life well lived? Satisfy and rectify this need to search, which until you do, is limiting your perspective on life. Then you can move on to a more peaceful, balanced, happy and productive life.

64. *Time to stop the repeating destructive patterns.*

How many times do you tell yourself "I can't" instead of "I Can"? When do you stop beating yourself up over past failures and mistakes? Do you see yourself falling for the same broken patterns of miserable relationships, or unsatisfying work choices? Do you make friends and then find yourself failing at being a 'good' supportive friend when they need you most? Do you let yourself down and give up quickly just before the finish line of a project. Do you tell yourself "this will never work" or "I am not good enough"? Look at the way you have been living your life and assess what has and hasn't happened so far for you. When you are caught in a loop of destructive patterns, often it is your thoughts that are keeping you on that particular Merry-Go-Round. When you decide it is time to reach for the brass ring and get off, your life will change for the better. If you can, sit still and think about the ways you constantly defeat yourself or ask a trusted friend what they see you doing over and over again that is keeping you stuck. Sometimes, just by being aware of what you are doing, you can make the changes necessary to stop the patterns. If the patterns are very deeply ingrained and troublesome then it is time to ask for help to break the cycle.

65. *Your path in life and who to follow is your choice!*

Yes, we are the centre of our own Universe. It has to be so, as it is up to us how we choose to live our life and create our reality. We also have the right to say, think, feel or act in a manner of our choosing. However, like interconnecting circles, we also flow and blend with each other while still remaining within our own independent space. Family, friends, co-workers and people of authority have the right to do and say things necessary for their own learning and growth as well. Sometimes though these same people feel they are doing it for the betterment of others. Their comments fill their own circle and surround them even while trying to draw us in and include or convince us of their beliefs. Their right to expression need not impinge on your rights or beliefs. When they think, say and do things in their own way, you at least know the truth of their thoughts. It doesn't mean you need to follow them or lose your sense of self. Allow others the freedom of their choices without debating your personal value because of them. Their actions and reactions belong to them, yet how we choose to interact is solely our choice.

66. Consider vulnerability to be a strength.

When we think of being vulnerable we think of being naïve, weak and open to hurt. We equate vulnerability with children and how impressionable, easily distracted and devastated they can become when life turns upside down. Yet think of how determined they can also become when facing a challenge, or told they cannot do something. Have you ever seen their expression of awe and wonder when they see a sunset or rainbow for the first time? Being open to experience whatever comes along without predisposed judgment about our abilities or where we fit in life is the only way we can learn and change direction when necessary. Life isn't meant to be judged in terms of good or bad, it is meant to be experienced through the good and bad to find out whom we really are inside. Being able to have that awe like wonder of the world, inquisitive nature to explore or try new things as well as the determination to try again when we hit a stumbling block, keeps us interested, engaged and connected to life. When you allow yourself those moments of flights of fancy, or take the opportunity to change your perspective, excitement, new relationships, job opportunities and so much more will seem to fall at your feet. Change your definition of vulnerability from one of pain and weakness to one of simply being open to learn, witness and experience life as a child.

67. *Look in the mirror.*

When was the last time you really looked in the mirror at yourself? For most it has been a long time since they made an assessment of what they see and who they have become. You are being asked to take that time now. Are there ways to improve your physical self such as letting go of extra pounds that have crept up over time? Are your muscles looking strong and toned? When you look at your posture, has it changed to one of slouching or defeat or do you stand proud, strong and tall? Take a look at the clothes you are wearing. What story would they tell someone you are meeting for the first time? Finally look directly into your eyes. Really ask yourself if they look happy and satisfied with life or are they filled with questions, pain or sadness. Can you tell yourself while focused and looking directly into your eyes that you love yourself right now? Go ahead and do it and see what happens. If this task isn't easy to do, and brings tears, discomfort or even silly laughter, reassess everything you have just witnessed in the mirror. Make the choice and take steps to change the things you can until who you see when you look into your eyes is a wonderful, happy and peaceful soul looking back.

68. Don't diminish or deny the value you add to life.

What do you think the world would look like if you were not in it? You, who just happen to be someone's child or parent, sibling, friend, neighbor, co-worker or boss. If you deny your existence you actually give others permission to ignore you as well. There is a very specific reason as to why you are here on earth at this time. Take time to look really hard inside yourself to discover the things you love or hate to do, gifts or talents unique to yourself, achievements and even failures. Learn from the past and move forward knowing there is always more to share or understand. There will always be those who could use a helping hand or those willing to lend you one. Get involved with others and stop hiding or being alone. Acknowledge the things that you admire in others and see what it would take for you to also own those skills or abilities. Look around you at the people in your life and see who depends on you or who comes to you for advice or just to chat. Pay attention to those who ask how you are doing or what is new. Even in the smallest way of offering a smile to a stranger or holding a door for someone whose arms are full or giving up your seat to someone who needs it more means you are adding value in no small way. What may seem like a small and insignificant gesture to you may mean the world to someone who has never been shown a kindness. In reality this can change their life.

69. Stop saying 'No', 'Not', or 'Never'.

Do you have difficulty changing a habit? For instance have you ever said, "I will never smoke again" only to find yourself almost immediately craving that last cigarette before you promise to 'never' do it, again? Never is said to be one of those words that the Universe as well as our subconscious self refuses to acknowledge.

In the same category you will also find: 'No' and 'Not'. These words seem to create a challenge in how long it will take to succumb to the issue we said we would 'not' do again. Telling yourself that you are 'Not' hungry when trying to change your eating habits leads to hunger pangs and cravings as the subconscious only hears 'I am hungry'. This part within each of us creates a file system of all that we have ever learned and experienced as well as the results from the challenges we have faced. This is why we can do things on auto pilot, like driving a car without consciously thinking of all the rules of the road, or baking cookies without having to find the recipe. To say that you will 'never 'do something, or are 'not' participating, or 'no', you won't, since it has yet to be established as a defined experience or base to offer support from, the subconscious can only offer what it does know. So when we say we will 'never' the subconscious only hears we 'will' and we then find ourselves acting according to what will happen and not what we think we are choosing 'not' to happen. Your words are creating your reality, so watch what you decree.

70. *Take the time now to re-activate your brain.*

Doing the same things over and over again in the same way denies the opportunity for change or growth. It sets up complacency in life where eventually boredom creates opportunity for bad habits to begin. Have you found yourself stuck in a rut lately? When was the last time you entered into a challenge or tried something new to excite and get you interested in life? How good are you at problem solving or working to complete jig saw puzzles? It is time to re-activate and exercise your brain. Make simple changes in your life such as brushing your teeth with the opposite hand, putting your

168

trousers on with the opposite leg first or eating with the other hand. Find word search books or cross-word puzzles, or find a hobby that brings satisfaction. The challenges do not have to be big ones at first. Master the small changes and the craving for something more challenging eventually will follow. Get up and shift your perception of the way things need to be done. You will then find yourself more engaged in life and more exciting to be around.

71. *Let your inner child come out to play.*

Our time here on earth is for learning, with earth being the biggest school house and duality in everything our biggest teacher. Where there is up there is down and where there is hot there is cold. We learn by constantly balancing ourselves between opposing forces and place ourselves where we are most comfortable. Even though there are bills to pay, work to be done, children to nurture and educate and so many serious things that take your time, there also needs to be time to have fun. This is the time to do the silly and fun things that make you laugh and forget time and cause your giggle muscles to hurt because you are laughing so hard. We all have within us a child like energy that does wish to have fun, needs to explore and have freedom of expression. When was the last time you had an ice cream cone just because, or got up and danced to some new moves just because you liked the beat of the music, or spontaneously invited people over for a movie night and passed around candy and popcorn? Have you tickled your partner or your children lately or gone out to fly a kite in a park or on the beach? These forms of childlike expression are healing and nurturing for your soul and are a natural way to release the stresses that the adult in us experiences. You are being asked to make it a routine to take the time and make the time to let loose and giggle.

72. Re-evaluate yourself.

Right now think about what you most admire about yourself. Was it difficult to do? Now think about what you are unhappy with when you focus on you. Was that easier? For most, they can recite at least 10 negatives for every positive thought identified. Always know that wherever you place your thoughts or focus, this is the reality that you will live through. For instance if your personal image that you see in the mirror brings you sadness or discomfort then you will find yourself hiding from social opportunities or even outings with friends. If you feel you lack in education then you will never challenge yourself to learn more because you will find yourself reverting to, "I am not smart enough to do that." Our shortcomings give us an easy excuse to remain where we are but also set limits on our ability and desire to explore life at any age. Even if your physical self was traumatized in some manner by birth, accident, emotion or illness, there are still ways to challenge yourself by using the strengths that seem to be overlooked. Identify your strongest assets; whether Physical, Intellectual, Creative, Emotional, Spiritual, Auditory, Keen sight and Observational skills or others that you know you have and realize these are your gifts to support you. Your shortcomings need not be the first thought when facing something new or different. When you own your strengths you just may find you will eventually learn to be at peace with the things about you that you cannot change, and then what can evolve will become a new confidence and strength. This new change in you may also be the inspiration to help another realize that they can also use their assets to change or support their self in their current reality.

73. Re-balance yourself.

What happens when you stand on just one foot for a few minutes, or walk or try to read with just one eye open? The answer is fatigue, strain on your body, constant focus and re-focus on staying upright or not bumping into things and falling over. This off balance state is what is currently happening in your life. Your life has become very one sided with work, family, health, finance or other of the major life stressors requiring your time and energy. The constant struggle to regain balance for moments of peace and contentment is wearing you out and clouding your vision of what you need in life. Even though these other things are real and current and need attention they are still just things or aspects of life. You also need and deserve time and attention. Make this moment of awareness an investment into yourself. Think about what needs to happen to bring back balance in your life and what that would look and feel like. Starting with just a few 'you' minutes each day will automatically direct your actions towards better health and wellbeing. Finding your balance also allows for clearer thought and more energy when needed to deal with the stressors we all face.

74. Do something just for you.

When was the last time you closed the door and deliberately placed a "do not disturb' sign on it? Never? Well it is time to place the focus entirely on you. Whether you meditate, do yoga, dance because no one is watching, journal, paint, or just sit and dream, make the time to separate yourself from your everyday world and concentrate on your interests, desires, or the small voice you can only hear when there is silence and peace within. When you show respect for yourself by deliberately stepping away from the world of phone, text, internet, email and TV or any other of a thousand and one distractions you will begin to see that others will become more respectful of you as well.

75. *Stop saying you are sorry just to keep the peace.*

What are you really sorry for? When you genuinely say you are sorry, you are taking ownership over your part in a situation that has affected the journey of another. This ranges from the simple act of bumping into someone, to hurting feelings and even causing devastating accidents. Being sorry then is an act of contrition where ownership over the act is valid and necessary and offers the opportunity for forgiveness to be given and received creating a rebalancing of energy. There are also times when you feel the grief, hurt, or pain for someone and are genuinely sorry they are going through such trying times. Then there are the times you say, Sorry, sorry, sorry, in your everyday conversation, when there is no genuine reason behind it. This takes ownership away from the parties responsible and inserts your energy needlessly. Think twice before saying you are sorry. Is there a reason that you are asking for forgiveness or offering comfort? Or has it become a catch word for you. The next time you say you are sorry ask yourself first what it is you are sorry for so that the word and energy it emits will be valued by those on the receiving end.

76. *Get real with your life.*

How visible are you within your own existence? Do you let your light shine by using your gifts and talents? Have you ever taken the time to discover the things you personally are good at? It is great to support others on their journey, yet we are all asked at some point in our lives to own the reason we are here on earth and explore our uniqueness and individuality. There is nothing more exciting and satisfying than finding something you are passionate about and working with this passion for your own pleasure. It is not always necessary to shake up the world with what you can do, yet the sense of deep inner peace when you connect with that specialness and greatness of who you are cannot be measured. Once you allow yourself to explore and work with this aspect of self, a confidence that you never knew you could have becomes natural. Who knows though, you just might end up adding something to this existence that no one else could have. It is time to get real with you.

77. Challenge yourself to do something outside the box.

Most lives have become structured timelines with bills to pay, family and friends to care for, obligations and commitments to meet, health to look after and so on. No matter how comfortable this existence is, it can eventually feel as if you are contained within a box. All of the rules for your existence are written on the inner walls. This could be the schedules for appointments as well as budgets and deadlines right there as part of the decoration, all the time in front of you without escape. At some point though this starts to feel so structured and routine that you may secretly look for a door to open simply to see what could be on the outside of the life you have created. This usually happens when you have metaphorically peeked through a window from inside your box and witnessed or heard voices talking about someone doing something with their life that maybe you had always wished to try. You also could possibly have awakened one morning from a dream where your subconscious presented a new potential reality. You are being asked to open that door and take a step outside the box and see what is perhaps written on the outside of those walls. The box you have created will still be there for your comfort and responsibility on your return, just challenge yourself to see what other opportunities are waiting on the outside.

78. *Put yourself in someone else's shoes to see life from a different perspective.*

Each of our own lives suits us since we created it as it is. Whether this life is of constant struggle, striving to achieve or peaceful, it is the life we have created, know, accept and understand. Even if there are times of discomfort, sorrow, confusion and stress, we still have put in place parameters and supports that we trust and can turn to. You are being asked at this time to look at life from a different perspective. If you have never faced a devastating health issue, how can you have compassion or understand the strain on finance, personal fatigue and fear as well as relationship issues for one who is? If you have never been disabled or gone anywhere blind or had your hearing taken away, how could you understand the difficulty in navigating on a daily basis? If you look the other way at the homeless, do you not understand that there is a potential for everyone to lose everything in a single moment and there but for the Grace of God you also could be? It is time to look at your life, be grateful for what you do have and then see life through the eyes of someone else. What are you thinking when presented with the thoughts of someone from a different walk of life? Do you think less of them and have judgement that if they had taken better care of themselves, saved their money, got an education, tried harder to find work , never became addicted or other defeating or limiting thoughts, then their life could have, would have, or should have been different? Or do you tend to ignore the plight of others, happy in the comfort of your own existence? There is another world of hurt and need out there and only by stepping out of your personal comfort zone and understanding or at least becoming aware of the life of another can you genuinely have compassion and see the duality that earth presents to us all. You are not being asked to live differently, just have understanding and compassion for those that do.

79. *Stop avoiding the real issues.*

Ok, so when was the last time you paid attention to that little twinge of discomfort or pain within your body? When did you last tell yourself that you should really go for a walk and then sit down again to watch TV? When your bills come in, do you cringe and know that you could be spending less, saving more and then look at the latest sale flyers anyway? It is time to look at the real issues in your life and stop escaping or ignoring them. What is at the bottom of this denial or avoidance of the realities in your life? What are you actually afraid of? Could it be that you are fearful of a major health issue and that is what is stopping you from seeking medical advice? Are you secretly angry with yourself for not being better off financially? How many friends have you walked away from because their lives seemed so much easier or they tried to give advice to make yours better when you complained one time too many? Today is the day, the first of the rest of your life to commit to facing up to the issues that you have been ignoring and actually do something about them or ask for help. This will ensure a happier and healthier future in all ways.

80. *Regrets make moving difficult, as if your feet are stuck in cement.*

It has been said that when we reach the end of our lives, we will never truly regret the things we did do but regret that we didn't take time for the things we wished we had done. It is a realization that occurs that whatever has happened in the past, there is no way to alter its existence or outcome. It happened, we did what we could, we were involved to the ability or level of commitment we had at the time and it is also beyond our capability to change whatever it was. When we hold onto our regrets we are actually placing our own feet in blocks of cement that hold us in place causing us to live our lives from that same feeling, frozen into a situation that can never be changed. It makes it so very difficult to move forward when we are still tied to the past. If you have regrets in this moment from anything that has already happened, take time to address this at least within yourself or with others that may have been involved if they are interested in closure. Not everyone is left with the same emotions or even recalls an experience the same way you do. We all have our own perspectives and what upsets one person, may only mildly aggravate another or not even cause a second thought to someone else. Look into your own feelings of regret and see if you can resolve and make peace within yourself by forgiving yourself or asking for forgiveness so you can free your feet to move forward into a better future.

81. *Are you actually listening to what is being said, or only what you wish to hear?*

There is the world of difference between listening and hearing. One may hear something and it is instantly dismissed or forgotten. The phrase that it has literally gone in one ear and out the other becomes a reality. When one actually takes the time to listen, it requires you to be still to absorb the information so that change can happen or opportunity can alter your path. Sometimes we have a preconceived notion of what someone is going to say to us and our ability to receive the information is skewed to match our perception of what we thought or would like to hear. The next time you are in a conversation with someone, really listen to what is being said as it is time for you to learn something about yourself and the life you are living.

82. *Take the time to check your posture.*

When was the last time you checked your posture? Do you stand strong, straight and tall, taking the full measure of the length of your spine and pulling those abdominal muscles in? Or, do you tend to slouch, with shoulders forward and abdomen drooping? Your posture tells a lot about how you engage in the world around you and how your physical body is dealing with stress. Medical science has proven through saliva hormone testing that the stress hormone called Cortisol, increases when a person stands in the defeated slouched position even for a short period of time. In energy work this position blocks the flow of fresh revitalizing energy causing fatigue and mental fog. It keeps one stuck in the fight or flight mode of survival. To stand straight and tall as a winner does when they cross the finish line strengthens the muscles along the spine and within the abdomen and realigns the chakras or energy centres. This opens the channel to allow for the old and potentially stagnant energy to be replaced and refreshed. Make the time to stretch yourself up every time you drink water or send a text message and declare to yourself that you are a winner and see how much happier and more energized you feel.

83. Love... What does it mean to you?

What is your definition of love? Is it something you freely give and share or something you have been protecting? Are you open about what and who you love or are you selective and private, holding the things you love near and dear within? Do you love conditionally or are afraid to love in case you get hurt? True love is an emotion based on faith, trust and confidence. However, it starts with loving oneself first. Only to the amount that you love, trust, accept and forgive yourself can you know when love is true coming from someone else. If we look at the reverse, it might be easier to say what love is not. It is not judgmental or conditional. It doesn't come with strings attached. It certainly isn't a commodity to be used for barter or exchange. Think of the things or people you love. Do you love them in spite of their strengths or shortcomings? Can you forgive their mistakes and lapses of memory when you feel forgotten or left out? Do you expect something in return when you say I love you? It is time to examine this emotion called love.

84. Hate? Is it holding you hostage?

What does it mean to hate? Children say they hate broccoli and turnip or an employee may say they hate their boss. At times when we are hurt, scared or challenged we cry out that we hate whoever or whatever is causing us distress. Some may feel that they hate a certain group of people, religion, organization or culture. Hate is a personal emotion and is the absence of all things caring, considerate, pleasurable and agreeable to oneself in a particular moment. The most destructive form of hate has fear or anger undertones. Hate can be fleeting and temporary as the child hating turnip may crave it as an adult. Hate can also be insidious and grow through mass consciousness where one person felt slighted or wronged and takes up a cause against something and then convinces others to join them in their fight for so called righteousness. The unfortunate part in that scenario is that not everyone in that group feels hate in the same way or to the same degree but gets caught up in the cause without truly understanding or first working to resolve or find peace within. Hate hurts us when we perpetuate the feeling by not forgiving or trying to understand what is making us feel this way. The last time you said you hated something, were you simply frustrated or refraining from seeking resolution or closure? To hate a food, a colour or type of music will never be life threatening but to hate another person, country, culture, group or religion has more ramifications on the person who hates than their perception for the reason to hate. You are being asked to face those things you have been saying you hate. See what resentments, fears, or unresolved angers you are repressing and find ways to seek peace. If they truly are deeply seated or overwhelming then ask for help. Hate when left unresolved will only grow and spread involving others in your battle. The person who continues to hate will always hurt the most. Make peace within yourself for your own health and wellbeing.

85. *What is really important to you?*

You are being asked to identify what is really important to you right now, today and in this moment. This is because life has a way of becoming routine, putting things we may like to do, really need to do or people in our lives on hold until we find a better time. We tell ourselves we are waiting until we finish something, have more money or time and then we will get to it. Importance is relevant to the individual. For some it is their health, or family. For others it could be education, taking a vacation, clearing debts or finding good and exciting relationships. There are so many important things in our lives yet there really is only one reality to address them in and that is this current moment in time. The past is simply just that, moments that we cannot change and time that we will never have again. Your future is undecided waiting for the investment you are currently making in this moment to create it. That only leaves today to appreciate, support, love or take care of what is most important in your life. Take the time to re-evaluate what is important and then take steps to address it today.

86. *Resentment, what does it mean to you?*

Resentment is one of the emotions that if allowed to take root, will grow over time into an ugly all consuming weed. It shuts out the light and stops any potential for growth as it takes over your thoughts and feelings. It may start with a simple misunderstanding that was never addressed, or a feeling that you were slighted or insulted. Maybe you resented being asked to do more work or put in overtime hours, or being volunteered for something as if you have no say in the importance of your time or ability to be involved. Resentment however can also be a shield to hide behind or an excuse to bring people to your side of an argument or disagreement. Ultimately resentment only limits the person resenting as the recipient on the other end of this emotion may be totally oblivious to their part of the issue. Whether it is towards a person, place or thing, identify what it is you resent and dig down to the root of it. Make the time to pull it out, examine it and make peace. By holding onto resentment you are ultimately only hurting yourself.

87. *Pay it forward.*

It has always been said that what goes around eventually comes around. Do you believe that by helping another you are ensuring support when you need help? Does assisting someone else feel so good that you want everyone to know you had a hand in their success? If this is the case it is time to think about assistance in a different light. A selfless act of support or kindness when done without expectation of reward or acknowledgement sets an energy in motion that reverberates through the Universe. Like ripples on a pond this carries unlimited potential for change. As long as those ripples are moving it doesn't matter what other ripples they interact with when the deeds offered are for the greater good. These selfless acts of kindness set their own ripples in motion creating a mindset of caring and support from the person receiving to then become the person of giving. What selfless good deed have you done for someone lately? Do something today to pay it forward for someone you don't even know and start a new set of positive and life affirming ripples. The Universe will thank you in ways you cannot even imagine.

88. Do your expectations end in disappointment?

So what did you expect? Why did you expect it? Those two questions always seem so hurtful when facing the disappointment of being unfulfilled in some manner. Expectation without an investment in preparation or action can lead to disappointment and dissolution. Have you ever been told that your expectations were unrealistic? The two words 'unrealistic expectations' often go together when others are trying to care for us or support us through some trauma where we entirely believed in a different outcome but hadn't really set things in motion to make it so. We set ourselves up for a world of hurt if we only expect things to happen without putting some effort into creating the result. To expect to win the lottery you have to at least go out and buy a ticket. To excel and be number one in your class you must study and put the effort into understanding the subject. To expect a good marriage or beautiful relationship requires an effort to understand the wants, needs, dreams and goals plus personality of the partner involved. To simply expect life to unfold the way you want it to is like asking for food in a restaurant. You will definitely receive something just not necessarily what you thought you wished for. Look at what you have been expecting to unfold in your life. Have you set the wheels in motion and invested any effort in making it happen?

89. Are you really helpless?

Do you believe that you are helpless? Do you really feel that you are lost, alone without any guidance, support or knowledge of how to get beyond the challenge you are now facing? The true definition of helpless is the state of having exhausted every avenue possible with no other ideas, options or opportunities remaining to change the undesired circumstance. You are being asked to reassess and look again at what is possible and not at what hasn't so far worked. You may need to ask for help to research other options, or talk to your doctor, therapist or find a religious or spiritual guide to give you direction. We are never given more than we can cope with if we make up our minds to never give up making an effort on our own behalf. You are stronger, smarter and with more resources than you know. Have faith, trust and keep going. You just may not be as helpless as you think. The solution really is there somewhere.

90. *The act of choice is so much more than wanting or needing brings.*

How often have you told yourself or others that you really need something? When questioned about this need do you then defend yourself by saying that yes, you absolutely want it? When working at manifesting things into our lives these two words; want and need can become a focal point for your thoughts and actions. If you think about it though, they can almost sound like pleading or whining. Within the act of manifesting, the words that you use are of vital importance as they give direction to a much bigger energy source where all answers and responses are sent from. So, when sending a request to the Universe to be made manifest, be more direct and say I 'choose', not I want or need. Stand in front of a mirror and watch yourself say, 'I want' and then repeat the phrase, 'I need'. How much strength can you really put behind those words? Now watch your face again as you say, 'I choose'. This action of choosing to receive carries the no nonsense directive that you are being clear with your request. By making a direct and clear choice you will not be left to understand the life lessons created when focused on needing or wanting.

91. *Intentions are stronger than hoping for something.*

What is it that you are hoping for? Do you hope to receive a raise or hope to meet that special someone? Do you hope to feel better tomorrow or hope to win the lottery? As much as we all live in hope of something better, when the results come in and they are not what we hoped for we are sent to the opposite end of this emotion into despair. When this happens we reset our hopes and send out a new thought or make the old one clearer while still relying on hope to make it happen. This act of hope is one of faith and through commitment and trust in due time, often these prayers are answered. However, if you change the act of 'hope' to one of 'intention' and get involved in taking whatever steps possible on your end to fulfill the 'hope' the answers may come that much faster and with more precision. An intention is about taking ownership and working alongside of the hope and not just sitting back and waiting. When an intention is put into motion it sends out strong ripples of energy into the Universe and like a magnet draws more of the same energy back to make it so. There may be times when hope is all there is left for a better tomorrow. Before that happens though examine what you are hoping for, and see if by changing the hope to an intention and working within it you can put stronger energy into manifesting that which you wish for.

92. *Are you expressing yourself clearly? What did you really mean to say?*

Are you saying what you mean and meaning that which you say? Do you find yourself fumbling over your words or get tongue tied when asked for an answer or suggestion? Do you think you have expressed yourself clearly only to hear your own words repeated but with a different context? You are being asked to pause before you offer a response and think of what your intention is in using the words and phrases you choose. Usually when speaking without thinking, it is more about defending previous choices or actions or trying to convince or control an outcome. It might also reflect a desire to appear smarter or be first to jump in to change the focus of a conversation back to a topic you are more comfortable with. There is a saying that once the words are out the barn door the fastest horse can never bring them back. If you have been speaking without thinking how your words will be received and if the meaning you intend to convey isn't clear then pause and take the time necessary to make your message clearer.

93. *What have you learned about life?*

As painful or exciting as our challenges may be we actually are here on earth to learn. If we don't voluntarily put ourselves in a position to see new perspectives or opportunities the Universe has a way of presenting new situations which forces us to do so. Think about the things that have always intrigued you and do some research to know more. Sign up for a course that challenges the way you think or have previously accomplished things. Join a group to share your knowledge and experience and be open to hearing differing viewpoints. Look at what you are uncomfortable with and ask yourself why? They say that the day we stop learning we die. You are being asked to get moving now and engage in something new.

94. *Are you hiding?*

What are you hiding from, or are you? If you really enjoy being on your own, then that is different from making excuses for not going out to join the world around you. If the pleasure of your own company satisfies and excites you and you can't wait to be with yourself every moment of every day then enjoy yourself. However, no man or woman is really meant to live in a void where when left alone there is limited progress, opportunity or change. We are here to engage in life as earth is experiential with duality wherever we look. Part of this experience is to overcome fears, share experiences, face challenges, or maybe even be an inspiration for someone else in some way. If you really are hiding by deliberately denying interaction with others and life in general then it is time to ask for help. Challenge yourself to come out of hiding, face fears, anxieties and deal with past hurts and indiscretions. Ask for or offer forgiveness, resolve issues, own up to mistakes and become more comfortable getting involved. Then when you are on your own you really can enjoy your own company.

95. *What are you really rebelling about?*

Do you find yourself pushing back, resisting change and being easily offended? When someone says you can't do something, do you say, watch me? Do you enjoy breaking the rules and defying authorities? There is a time and place within this existence to stretch the limits and explore possibilities and argue to defeat theories or outdated protocols and societal mores. There is though a huge difference when the intent is to be deliberately difficult, obnoxious, rude, insulting and belligerent just for your own fun and the attention it brings to you. If you have that much energy and desire to be annoying look to see what is driving you to rebel. What is forcing you to take this attitude toward life? Rebelling after a while becomes stale and self serving and eventually pushes those who love you and the ones you need away. Look at your rebellion and acts of defiance as a wakeup call and challenge to heal and find inner peace. Be open to new ideas and let yourself learn more about what makes you real. Stop acting out against life and find a way to retain your uniqueness and put your challenging nature to use making a difference and not just a disturbance.

96. *What are you really hungry for?*

When was the last time you went to the fridge, opened the door and stood there lost because you knew you wanted something but couldn't figure out just what it was? Or, did you turn on the TV and flip through the channels not finding anything that grabbed your attention? Have you ever made a phone call because you thought hearing another voice might be the answer to a vague hunger for something? Hunger is actually a request from your inner self to identify a specific need, or to address what isn't working in your life, seeking resolution to achieve that satisfied feeling. There are the usual categories one might hunger for such as, and not limited to: dietary sustenance, satisfying relationships, financial stability, healthy body image and wellbeing, further education or more positive career choices. There can also be the ones of addiction when an unhealthy craving for more of what sabotages, keeps us from looking too deeply at what the hunger really represents. Once you can identify what you really are hungry for by asking what is missing, broken or wrong in your life, it takes an act of deliberate intent to find a way to satisfy that particular drive or craving. Get help if the hunger is deep or debilitating. Hunger for something represents an emptiness waiting to be filled.

97. *Do you let anyone get close to you or enter your inner circle?*

What is your social circle like? Do you openly share your life stories or do you put up a wall and if someone gets too interested or friendly do you retreat behind it? Would people say that you would rather hear the sound of your own voice or are you a good listener and support? Do you set up a series of road blocks as a test to see who is willing to run the gamut to be worthy of you as a friend? It is next to impossible to function solely without interconnected relationships and trust in our lives. Ask yourself how you define friendship and what qualities you have to offer. To have a close friend you must be a close friend. However, you must first be a friend to yourself. Are you happy with your own company? What can you offer to create honest and lasting bonds with people? Letting someone into your inner circle doesn't mean that you will never suffer disappointment within that relationship. However, from every interaction we allow ourselves to experience, we learn more about who we are so that we become stronger, wiser and more interesting when the next offer of friendship is presented.

98. *Healing from Grief and Loss is possible.*

During that time in life when we have lost someone or something that we loved and or depended on, the devastation we feel is very real. Whether it is a person, pet, place, something valuable or sentimental or even a career, time seems to stand still. In that moment of despair, emptiness and hurt, it is difficult to breathe, or think about any of the daily and mundane functions we would normally do. This is a natural response to shock or trauma. It is also absolutely necessary to spend the time to remember, before we can make peace with the pain and changes that come from this unhappy and often seemingly cruel aspect of life. There will also come a time when you will be offered opportunities to rejoin the current world and start to function again. No one can say how long grief or loss should last. These emotions are as individual as the designs are on snowflakes. Yet the one commonality that everyone who has suffered must face, is life constantly knocking at your door, asking if you are ready yet to be nurtured by those willing to help you heal. Although grief is a solitary journey there are others who have trudged down that lonely, sad and hurtful path and found a way through the dark, dense forest back to the fields of flowers and sunshine. When you are ready you will hear the knocking. When you do, open the door and let a little of that fresh air and light come in where there has been nothing but darkness. Life will go on either with or without your permission. Allow your self to be drawn back in and although the memories will remain the intensity of the hurt and pain will gradually diminish over time. Once you have found your field of flowers in the sun, as you allowed yourself to be helped, you might also be the one who helps another out of that dark dense place you came to know so well.

99. Let go of jealousy as it will eat away at your self-worth.

Are you satisfied and happy with where you are right now in life? When you look at your family, neighbors and friends do you find it within you to applaud and celebrate their successes and equally share in their sorrows? Yeah you, if those feelings and abilities to participate are genuine. You see there is another side to life that may occur when you start to compare lives. The term is jealousy which is really an excuse for not working harder on your own existence to make it better in some way. To define this emotion one has only to ask if you have ever been upset because someone you know just bought a new car and you wonder bitterly how they can afford it. Or when invited to see the pictures of the amazing vacation of a friend, do you make excuses not to go? Do you find it difficult and resent having to meet the new love in someone's life? Jealousy or envy eats away at happiness and the ability to see clearly what needs to happen in your own life to make it better. For some it seems easier to beat themselves up over the lack they feel in their lives compared to others, than to do the work necessary to create the same or better circumstance for their self. Are you being envious or jealous and feeling slighted and unlucky? Stop comparing and take action to make your own life happier.

100. Volunteer to help others and commit to doing a selfless act.

There is a saying that the best way to heal ourselves and move through our own trials is to go out and offer to help another. You are being asked to step outside of your own issues or comfort zone and experience the world through the life and challenges of someone or something else. You could offer to read stories to children in a school, at the library or in a hospital. You could assist with the preparation of food or serving of the less fortunate in a food kitchen. You could also work with seniors in a home or animals at a shelter. There are so many places needing people like you to offer your time and personal presence. The opportunity to learn so much more about life and yourself from the experience is invaluable. Take time to share the gifts, wisdom and that unique and individual piece of yourself solely for the purpose of making someone else feel special, not forgotten, stupid or without value. When you do it as an act of charity, freely given, the understanding you will gain for your own life is immeasurable.

101. *Are you a patient person?*

Patience is a lost art form. In this age of instant everything we forget that we must still follow earths linear timeline of cause and effect, work and reward and so many other of the dualities that we came to experience. For example, it is really unrealistic to achieve 'instant' weight loss by following a new diet plan or way of combing foods. If weight loss is the challenge, the gain in weight did not happen in an 'instant' so why would we expect it to leave that quickly. Our bodies need time to readjust, heal and find a healthy balance. To find the man or woman of your dreams ringing your doorbell although it can happen, again is not a result based on reality. To find that special someone we are asked to set things in motion such as joining a new social circle or getting involved in a project we love so that the opportunity to meet new people is more likely to occur. Many people pray for patience during trying and painful times, and yet it isn't a commodity that one can be handed just because they ask for it. Patience is actually a virtue that once acquired through deliberately getting out of the way and allowing life to unfold eventually becomes a strength and comfort. The art of patience requires practice like building the strength in a muscle through observation and non-judgement. Remove yourself from demanding immediate results when faced with a challenge and the rewards will be more than you can imagine.

About The Author

Hi, My Name Is Helen:

I began my career as a Registered Technologist in Diagnostic Radiography in 1972. While working in the medical field, over time, I began to realize that there was more to healing than isolating and treating individual parts of the body. I found that our thoughts, beliefs and attitudes played a distinctive role in our health and happiness.

By trying to resolve issues in my own life, my journey led me into the spiritual realm of personal responsibility, and the studies of Alternative Health Care.

I have been a Reiki Master since 1997, and completed my family counseling studies in 2003. During that time I also completed advanced levels of Crystal Healing Therapy, Metamorphic Technique and Ear Candling. I then felt drawn to study hypnosis through to the Masters level of Hypnotherapy at the Ontario Hypnosis Guild, and to further achieve my Masters registration in Hypnosis in Canada and with the American Medical and Dental Association. These studies have helped me to understand the role our subconscious plays in decision making and responses or reactions to various life situations.

With my Spiritual understanding and studied knowledge of Energy work, I was guided to share and teach by organizing many types of workshops and retreats. Women's weekends, co-facilitating crystal healing retreats, plus spiritual energy training and workshops, plus my own private mentoring work, were only a few of the very successful methods that I have used, to help others move forward into joy, peace and balance.

A few years ago I felt challenged to find deeper answers for my clients to the questions of "Why do these things happen to me?" and "What do I need to understand?" "Why do I feel stuck" and "Why do I continue to repeat the same mistakes?" Through my trust and faith in the Universe, I was guided to write the Channeled Resources found in this book.

I welcome the opportunity to share this Channeled Work with my readers to provide different perspectives and potential answers as to why things happen in our lives. This work will also assist in understanding and releasing some of the more troubling issues from the past and present that we face from time to time, allowing you to find peace and joy in the life you lead.

I wish you all the best on your journey.

www.ingramcontent.com/pod-product-compliance
Lightning Source LLC
Chambersburg PA
CBHW080529090426
42733CB00015B/2524